Al Jazeera and the DoD: The Need for Greater Engagement

In the wake of a horrific tsunami that has devastated a sizeable portion of the island of Sumatra, the world watches in horror as the massive Indian Ocean wave recedes taking with it entire villages and thousands of inhabitants. The grievous loss of life and pervasive destruction in Sumatra has not only crippled the country of Indonesia, but it has also triggered widespread pandemonium throughout the entire Asian Pacific as citizens and politicians become gripped with fear.

Racing to assist its Indonesian ally, a U.S. Joint Task Force (JTF) prepares to undertake the massive humanitarian relief operation with the most noble of intentions and with an expectation that every action will be intensely scrutinized by a watchful international audience and an even more apprehensive Indonesian public. Knowing the strategic implications of an increased U.S. presence in the Indian Ocean and the mixed signals it may send to both allies and adversaries, the JTF commander recognizes the critical importance of communicating the goals and the intentions behind the operation to the global audience and most importantly, to the Indonesian people. To prepare for this challenge, the JTF commander has directed her staff to invite several international television news networks to provide embedded reporters for the duration of the operation. Given the limited access and flow of information from the devastated area, the media networks graciously accept the invitation, most notably *Al Jazeera-Asia*, the newest of the many *Al Jazeera Network* channels. As quickly as the announcement is made of the JTF's movement toward Sumatra, Jemaah Islamiah, one of several transnational Islamic terrorist organizations present in Indonesia, begins a widespread propaganda campaign to discredit the operation. Utilizing its web-based media platforms and access to satellite television, the terrorist's spokesman boldly proclaims the tsunami was actually caused by the U.S. in an effort to occupy Indonesia and to destroy Islam. Issuing a fatwa on *Twitter,* the terrorist leader denounces the U.S.-led effort and calls for global jihad to prevent the U.S. force from reaching its intended target. Within minutes, the terrorist's "tweet" reaches millions of followers and is "re-tweeted" to millions more from Asia, Africa, Europe, the Middle East and North America. Professionally- edited videos showing U.S. atrocities in both Iraq and Afghanistan begin to populate *You Tube* warning viewers of the result of U.S. occupation in Muslim countries. Graphic images from those same videos begin to populate other social media platforms further increasing the confusion and trepidation of the JTF's presence in the Indonesian waters. Unlike previous operations, the JTF is prepared for this type of "information warfare" and "social media swarm".[1]

Leveraging its team of public affairs (PA) specialists to rapidly distribute imagery, videos and *tweets* that showcase ongoing rescue operations, medical care, and food distribution, the JTF also shares many of these products with the embedded media networks. One piece of video that is particularly striking is a helmet- cam video from a U.S. Navy petty officer as he rescues two children from the strong currents and floating debris of the tsunami's flood waters. The video draws the attention of the *Al Jazeera* crew and upon approval of the JTF commander, *Al Jazeera* is allowed to use the video clip. Meanwhile, the JTF commander agrees to conduct a live remote interview with *Al Jazeera-Asia through* its regional media hub in Jakarta. Witnessing some of the first footage of both the disaster and the relief operation, 200 million viewers across the globe tune in to watch *Al Jazeera's* exclusive program including the raw but captivating rescue footage and the live interview with the U.S. commander in charge of the operation.

Drawing confidence from her vast experience in similar operations and her multiple assignments within the Asian-Pacific, she astutely addresses each question with deep insight and expertise of not only the military mission, but also the Indonesian geography, history and culture as well. Assuring the world and Indonesian people of the JTF's intent, the commander affirms the U.S. military's commitment to providing relief and support to the Indonesian people. When asked about the terrorist allegations of U.S. occupation and atrocities, she calmly rebuffs the allegations by reminding the audience of the U.S. military's prior contributions to humanitarian relief in the Pacific as well as the extensive and enduring bilateral relationship that has existed between the Indonesian and U.S. military forces for over 60 years. She concludes the interview by thanking the global community, in particular the Asian-Pacific Alliance that has provided a broad base of support to the operation.

Her non-combative style, vast knowledge of the strategic setting and clear articulation of the JTF's intent not only informs the global audience, but it also assuages most of the world's concerns and clearly counters the terrorist propaganda both in words and images. What makes the interview so intriguing and effective is not just the character of the commander or the clarity of the message, but in this case it is also the credibility of the network with the worldwide Muslim audience.

Although this scenario is fictitious; it highlights just one of countless security complexities facing the U.S. military and its leadership both in the present day and in the foreseeable future. Complexities distinguished by an evolving and easily accessible global information network and a chaotic and highly competitive news environment. Because of this rapidly expanding phenomenon, military actions and operations will be conducted under increased media scrutiny and will require greater transparency especially for the international audience. Additionally, U.S. military operations within the Middle East will be widely scrutinized by a global Muslim audience, who has become more distrustful and critical of U.S. policies and military strategy. As such, this necessitates greater engagement with international news networks by the U.S. Department of Defense (DoD) and its military services. In particular, the *Al Jazeera Network* represents one of the fastest growing and most influential news networks among the myriad media who dominate the global information environment.

This research provides a historical perspective of the foundations and growing influence of the *Al Jazeera Network* and its wide variety of channels, while also examining its relationship with the DoD. Although there have been countless publications that focused on *Al Jazeera* and its relationship with the U.S., this research is the first to focus exclusively on *Al Jazeera's* relationship with the DoD, examine its implications and recommend a way forward. As a result of the findings of this research, there appears to be growing need for greater engagement by the DoD and the Joint Services with the *Al Jazeera Network* and a need for increased exposure to the network and its affiliated channels by the DoD and its public affairs specialists.

Author's Note: For reader clarity and conciseness, the *Al Jazeera Network* will be referred to as *Al Jazeera* and any of its subordinate channels will be distinguished by the use of a hyphen following the *Al Jazeera* name (i.e. *Al Jazeera-Arabic*, *Al Jazeera-English*)

I. *Al Jazeera*'s Rise to Global News Provider

With the recent decision by *Al Jazeera* to purchase Current TV[2], the network took a significant step in reaching beyond the Middle East and into American living rooms. In a January 2, 2013 news release, *Al Jazeera* Director General Ahmed bin Jassim Al Thani said, "By acquiring Current TV, *Al Jazeera* will significantly expand our existing distribution footprint in the U.S., as well as increase our newsgathering and reporting efforts in America. We look forward to working together with our new cable and satellite partners to serve our new audiences across the U.S."[3] The newly created, *Al Jazeera* America will be headquartered in New York City and expects to operate from bureaus and new offices in several US cities while doubling its US-based staff to more than 300 employees.[4] With this acquisition, *Al Jazeera* now has the ability to compete with other U.S. cable television networks for its share of American viewership and global credibility. The business agreement also serves as a dramatic indicator of the expansion of one of the world's most controversial yet least understood television networks; a network whose origins can be traced back to 1995 in Doha, Qatar.

In June 1995, Sheikh Hamad bin Khalifa Al Thani seized control from his father for the leadership of the nation of Qatar through a bloodless coup d'état. Considered by many as an innovative and progressive leader for his efforts to modernize the Qatari military and relying heavily on the advice and ideas from young, Western-educated advisers, Sheikh Hamad sought to increase the small Gulf State's international influence and esteem through a wide variety of social, technological, economic, and political reforms within Qatar. [5] Chief among these was the abolishment of the Qatari Ministry of Information, a long-standing institution charged with publicity and censorship of the press within Qatar. Sheikh Hamad's decision to eliminate the institution responsible for promoting the ideals and interests of the state marked a major divergence from most Middle Eastern nations and rulers. Shortly after this, Sheikh Hamad issued a decree in February 1996 calling for the financial support of a news network that would be the first independent satellite news network in the Middle East. By providing a loan of roughly $137 million for a five year period vice a direct subsidy, Sheikh Hamad and the Qatari Government effectively distanced themselves from direct oversight of the editorial content of the fledgling news channel now dubbed *Al Jazeera* or "The Island". [6]

On November 1, 1996 *Al Jazeera* began broadcasting from its headquarters in Doha, Qatar and since that time, *Al Jazeera* has grown into the Middle East's largest and most influential television network. According to Dr. Shawn Powers, a renowned expert on the international media and the Middle East, there were three factors that fueled *Al Jazeera*'s success: "its mission and financial support, its commitment to hiring professional journalists with in-depth local knowledge, and access to international communications equipment." [7] Leveraging the generous Qatari financial support and a well timed decision by the *British Broadcasting Corporation (BBC)* to cease its endeavor to launch an Arabic version of its news channel, *Al Jazeera* quickly found a void in 24 hour news coverage being broadcast from the Middle East and the quality of reporters and production of that news. Well trained and educated reporters, who had aspired to work for the newly formed *BBC- Arabic* television network, suddenly found themselves out of work. *Al Jazeera* offered them not only employment, but also an opportunity to become pioneers in this ground-breaking endeavor. According to authors Mohammed

El Nawawy and Adel Iskandar in their historical account of *Al Jazeera*: "The staff was trained in the Western journalistic tradition; wielding the expert knowledge and understanding of Arab politics and audiences, they were the final ingredient in the recipe for *Al Jazeera*'s eventual success."[8] Additionally, *Al Jazeera*'s securing of space on the Arabsat (a Saudi owned communications satellite) provided the network with access to the only satellite broadcasting throughout the Middle East at that time. This afforded *Al Jazeera* the opportunity to reach thousands more households and enabled the network to transform from a terrestrial-based news network broadcasting only six hours a day to a 24 hour a day satellite news network. Most media experts would agree this access was key to *Al Jazeera*'s rapid ascension and its ability to reach across the Middle East and beyond.[9] *Al Jazeera's* formation and editorial freedom proved to be a significant step towards greater media independence within the Middle East, a region that had long been host to state-owned or regime-sponsored media.

Al Jazeera consists of multiple channels and support entities including:

Channel	Description	Established
Al Jazeera-Arabic	Original *Al Jazeera* 24 hour news channel broadcasting in Arabic only	November 1996
Al Jazeera-Sport	Wide variety of sports channels broadcast in multiple languages	Ranging from 2003 to 2012
Al Jazeera-Mubasher (Live)	Live political and government focused channel broadcast in Arabic	2005
Al Jazeera-Mubasher Misr (Egypt Live)	Live political and government focused channel broadcast in Arabic focused on Egypt	2011
Al Jazeera-English	Largest of *Al Jazeera's* channels featuring global 24 hour news coverage in English	2006
Al Jazeera-Documentary	Channel dedicated to the presentation of documentary films, especially focused on political, historical, or social issues and broadcast in Arabic	2007
Al Jazeera-Children's Channel	Children's programming (ages 6-15) consisting of animated and live action shows either in Arabic or broadcast with Arabic voiceovers.	2005
Al Jazeera-Balkans	Broadcast from Sarajevo, Bosnia and Herzegovina focused on the Balkans in Bosnian/Croatian/Serbian language(s)	2011
Al Jazeera-Turk	Broadcast from Istanbul, Turkey focused on Turkey and regional countries in Turkish language	Pending 2013
Al Jazeera-America	Headquartered in New York City focused on both American domestic issues and international news in English	Pending 2013
Al Jazeera Media Training and Development Center	Based in Doha, Qatar focused on both practical and scientific implications of media in various fields and levels for *Al-Jazeera* network employees and others in the media field.	2004

Al Jazeera Public Liberties and Human Rights Department	Focused on promoting respect for human rights and public liberties by monitoring, documenting, broadcasting and raising awareness for these key issues in the world as a whole and in the Arab region in particular.[11]	2008
Al Jazeera Center for Studies	*Al Jazeera*'s "Think tank", conducts in-depth analysis of current affairs at both regional and global levels.	2006

Al Jazeera-Arabic was the first of the many channels now broadcasting as part of the *Al Jazeera Network.* Initially developed as an Arabic language news and current affairs channel focused principally on Middle Eastern issues and events, the channel also covers concerns and perceived injustices across the globe. Broadcasting from its Doha-based headquarters, it has garnered most of the world's attention for its highly critical and somewhat controversial style of television journalism, including video, talk shows and commentaries that evoke strong emotions and heated debate among its guests and its viewers.

Al Jazeera-English was launched in November 2006 coinciding with *Al Jazeera's* ten year anniversary and was intended to provide global news coverage to the English speaking world. Dr. Shawn Powers saw *Al Jazeera-English*'s goals as twofold: "(1) to meet a growing demand for accurate, timely news about the Middle East and other underrepresented parts of the world that could be delivered to English-speaking audiences; (2) to launch a global news network on par with the world's most prestigious news organizations that would, as a result of its association to and generous support from Qatar, help generate goodwill toward the small Gulf State, particularly in the West."[12] Six years since its first broadcast, *Al Jazeera-English* has become widely recognized as a leading competitor with the likes of *CNN International* and *BBC World*. Professor Seib also offered: "In some ways the English-language channel is more interesting than its Arabic sibling because the potential audience is so much greater for the English channel than for the Arabic one."[13]

Al Jazeera-Mubasher and *Al Jazeera-Mubasher Misr* both feature live and unedited coverage in Arabic of political, social, and cultural events throughout the Middle East and Egypt respectively. Similar to the U.S. based *C-SPAN*, both channels cover newsworthy conferences and events without commentary.

Al Jazeera-Documentary is principally designed to offer high quality documentaries focused on a variety of topics of interest to the Arabic speaking viewers including: political, cultural, historical, social, and artistic matters. The channel claims that it will produce 15% of broadcast material in-house, while obtaining the rest from Arab and global producers. Programs ranging from the evolution of food in the 21st Century, the myths behind Scientology, and the seeds of the Egyptian Revolution are offered in either programmed live broadcasts or in "on demand" streaming video. [14]

The *Al Jazeera Children's Channel* typically broadcasts 18-19 hours a day and produces around 40 percent of its own programs, a significantly higher percentage than most children's programming. Managed by the Qatar Foundation for Education, Science and Community Development, a Qatari nonprofit organization focused on education, science and community development, the channel's main objective is to enrich children's lives with quality programming and multimedia content that educates, informs and entertains. In addition to its normal programming that includes live interactive programs, competitions and games, news, sports and scientific magazine-style programs for a variety of age groups, the channel recently inked a deal with Disney to begin broadcasting its programming as well."[15]

Al Jazeera Balkans provides 24-hour television news coverage in the Balkans and although it is based in the Bosnian capital, Sarajevo, it also operates smaller news offices in Serbia, Macedonia and Croatia. Broadcasting in Serbo-Croatian language as well as local languages, the channel was created to provide a broader and more objective approach to news coverage within the region.[16]

Al Jazeera-Turk is scheduled to begin broadcasting from its headquarters in Istanbul at some point in 2013. Seeking access to the Turkish speaking audiences around the world, *Al Jazeera* acquired the Cine 5 television channel for $40.5 million in February 2011 with the expectation to begin broadcasting at some point in that same year. However, conflict with the Turkish Government over specific language used in identifying the Kurdistan Workers Party (PKK) seems to have brought the channel's launch to a standstill.[17]

Al Jazeera-America is slated to begin broadcasting later this year although no formal date has yet been set. *Al Jazeera*'s plan is to "build a distinctively US channel for American viewers with 60 percent of the content produced locally and 40 percent coming from *Al Jazeera-English*, their global network."[18] According to *Al Jazeera*'s press release, "*Al Jazeera*'s decision to create a U.S. based news channel was based in part on the fact that Americans have already shown a great demand for its news and programs: Almost 40 percent of all online viewing of *Al Jazeera*-English comes from the

United States."[19] However, the channel's entry into the American cable television race has been met with mixed reactions and support from across the country.[20] Enabled by the sale of *Current TV* cable network for $500 million, the newest *Al Jazeera* channel will be headquartered in New York City and recently posted job openings for some 100 new positions within its headquarters and in Washington, DC. [21] In addition to New York City and Washington, DC, the channel is planning on using existing *Al Jazeera-English* news bureaus in Miami, Los Angeles and Chicago while also expanding to other U.S. highly populated cities.

As early as 2010, the *Al Jazeera Media Training and Development Center* had provided more than 750 training courses for some 7,500 trainees from a variety of Middle Eastern countries, Europe, the United States, and Asia.[22] Partnerships with organizations like The International Center for Journalists and Harvard University's Program on Humanitarian Policy and Conflict Research provide ample opportunities for training and education of the next generation of global journalism professionals.

Established in 2006, the *Al Jazeera Center for Studies* represents *Al Jazeera*'s "think tank" on a wide variety of topics ranging from current affairs to global issues. With a network of researchers and experts from around the world, the center is highly regarded among other Middle East-based think tanks. Its research agenda focuses principally on addressing geo-political challenges such as Iran and Turkey's foreign policy with Egypt as well as the future of the economic landscape within the Middle East post-2015.[23]

The establishment of the *Public Liberties and Human Rights Department* in 2008 also gives *Al Jazeera* a powerful voice in the prevention of human abuse and the call for humanitarian intervention. Headed by Sami Al Hajj, an *Al Jazeera* journalist who was arrested in December 2001 by Pakistani Security Forces as a suspected Al Qaeda operative and was later detained at Guantanamo Bay for six and a half years by the United States[24], the department is held in high esteem among the senior *Al Jazeera* leaders as evidenced by the statement of Wadah Khanfar, the former Director General of *Al Jazeera* on the establishment of the department: "This important *Al Jazeera* initiative will promote respect for public liberties and highlight the need for basic human rights for all individuals throughout the Middle East and the rest of the world. Broadcasting and promoting those values will create an incentive for their respect and fulfillment among all those reached by *Al Jazeera*'s media network."[25]

With this wide variety of programming, increased markets and the support of its training and education centers, *Al Jazeera* is continuing to expand its influence and impact on the global media industry as well as in many of the newest international journalists.

***Al Jazeera*'s Growing Audience**

Although exact audience numbers are hard to determine, recent publications have estimated over 260 million households have daily access to *Al Jazeera* programming.[26] *Al Jazeera-English* alone claims to reach "more than 220 million households in more than 100 countries."[27] *Al Jazeera-English* was launched in November 2006 coinciding with the ten year anniversary of *Al Jazeera Media* and was intended to provide global news coverage to the English speaking world. *Al Jazeera-America* is slated to begin broadcasting later this year although no formal date has yet been set. *Al Jazeera's* plan is to "build a distinctively US channel for American viewers with 60 percent of the content produced locally and 40 percent coming from *Al Jazeera-English*, their global network." [28] With the establishment of *Al Jazeera-America*, the *Al Jazeera* global audience could potentially exceed 300 million this year. Comparing these figures with viewership data from 2006, this represents a 400% increase in the *Al Jazeera* audience in just a six year period of time.[29]

Al Jazeera has expanded its web-based media presence as well. In 2012, the *Al Jazeera-English* website received over 150 million visits with more than 40 percent of all visits coming from the United States. Utilizing high quality streaming videos and citizen-based video footage on its own websites, as well as a You Tube channel that boasts a combined 55 million plus channel viewers, *Al Jazeera* continues to dramatically increase its audience base and appeal.[30] In the area of social media, *Al Jazeera-English* is also one of the most "retweeted" news channels in the world, indicating a high amount of trust from the *Al Jazeera* audience for those who use *Twitter*.[31] *Al Jazeera*'s *Twitter* and *Facebook* fans constitute an additional 13 million followers of the network's various programs.[32] *Al Jazeera-English* also far outdistances its competitors in its use of *Twitter*, considered by many as the most popular form of social media today. As of March 2013, *Al Jazeera-English* had "tweeted" over 87,000 times and had over 1.6 million followers, nearly doubling the amount of "tweets" and followers of *CNN International*.[33]

With over 200,000 web views a month, new cutting edge programming like "The Stream" features an interactive dialogue that leverages social networking sites like *Twitter*, *Facebook*, *Instagram*, *Pinterest* and *Google Plus* to generate instant audience-based commentary and feedback. Highly popular among the young and educated international audience, it covers topics ranging from "how Israelis perceive Iranians" to "how Americans view gun control." "The Stream" has gained widespread popularity across the globe from a new generation of *Al Jazeera* viewers in just a little over a year.[34]

Al Jazeera's dramatically expanding audience coupled with its highly visual programming and web-based platforms have transformed the network from regionally focused news provider to a true global news leader.

***Al Jazeera*'s Founding Principles and Controversy**

Stemming from its desire to be "an independent and non partisan satellite TV network free from government scrutiny, control, and manipulation"[35] and its desire to adhere to its foundational principles, no other television network's name evokes more emotion than *Al Jazeera* does today. Since its inception, *Al Jazeera* has been hailed by world leaders for its independent and non partisan coverage of global issues yet hated by those same leaders for its coverage of domestic news stories within their respective countries. In reviewing multiple publications and *Al Jazeera* programming it is apparent their editorial principles are guided by three themes for reporting: present the "opinion and the other opinion," serve as a "voice for the voiceless," and focus reporting on "south to north"

From its earliest beginnings, *Al Jazeera* has sought to be an "open-minded" global news provider with a uniquely Arab perspective free from the filter of Western influence and governmental oversight including its main financier, Qatar. To help achieve this, the network adopted the motto "the opinion and the other opinion" and created programs that were designed to stimulate debate and controversy. According to Edmund Ghareeb, an expert in Middle Eastern affairs, "*Al-Jazeera* has helped satisfy a hunger in the Arab world. Its debate and discussion programs are tumultuous even by Western standards. They cover Arab issues in depth and with passion, by offering guests who include government and opposition figures, and who debate taboo issues such as secularism and religion."[36] Even in topics previously only covered from one perspective by Arab media, namely the Palestinian-Israeli conflict, *Al Jazeera* offered both sides the opportunity to present their viewpoints and perspectives on its different programs.[37]

Al Jazeera also sought to become "the voice of the voiceless" as it highlighted many of the ills of society and the lives of those who suffered as a result. Avoiding the commentary and public statements bordering on government propaganda, *Al Jazeera* sought to bring out the human interest perspective of every story including civilian casualties from war, starving families in refugee camps, and widowed spouses of police officers. In a recent episode aired on *Al Jazeera-English's* "Fault Lines", the channel highlighted the growing threat of violence in the city of Anaheim, California while another show focused on a newlywed couple of Syrian rebels fighting together on the front lines in Aleppo, Syria. Both stories continue to highlight *Al Jazeera's* desire to remain the "voice for the voiceless".

Al Jazeera has also elected to focus its news coverage on stories from what they coin as "the Global South" or those areas of the world that are typically underreported such as the Middle East, Africa, Asia and Latin America. In reviewing the *Al Jazeera* websites, users will typically see stories from these areas of the world in much greater prevalence than other global news networks.

***Al Jazeera*'s Love- Hate Relationship with the World and its Leaders**

Unfortunately for *Al Jazeera*, its editorial values have not always been appreciated by its viewers and embraced by governments across the globe. Beginning with the Middle East, *Al Jazeera* challenged many of the ruling parties and their policies in the areas of corruption, human rights and censorship through its news casts and current affairs talk shows. As presenters, guests and viewers openly debated many of these issues with greater fervor and frequency, *Al Jazeera* soon found itself under attack from all sides. When *Al Jazeera* opened its studio and programs to interviewing Israeli officials, some claimed *Al Jazeera* was part of a larger Zionist conspiracy to control the media. "Others whispered that it was controlled by the Muslim Brotherhood[38], pointing to the prominence in its religious programming of Yusuf Qaradawi, an Egyptian cleric with past links to the group. Numerous governments alarmed with *Al Jazeera* granting airtime to their opponents, clamped restrictions on its reporters and warned advertisers to spend their money elsewhere."[39]

Labeled as biased by some and blessed by others, *Al Jazeera's* popularity seemed to shift on a daily basis depending on the news story of the day. In fact, at one point every single Arab country had complained to Qatar about *Al Jazeera*. Some chose to recall their ambassadors and others closed down *Al Jazeera's* bureaus within their respective countries. But Qatar's foreign minister, Sheik Hamad Bin Jasim Al-Thani believed Al-Jazeera was doing something good for the Middle East during a 2001 interview with *CBS News' 60 Minutes*; "We are giving the people around us, in the Arab world, something which they need." [40]

Middle East scholar and author, Marc Lynch credits *Al Jazeera* for ushering in "a new kind of open, contentious public politics in which a plethora of competing voices clamored for attention… conclusively shattered the state's monopoly over the flow of information, rendering obsolete the ministries of information and the oppressive state censorship that was smothering public discourse well into the 1990s….The new public has forced Arab leaders to justify their positions far more than ever before, introducing a genuinely new level of accountability to Arab publics."[41] The accountability was not always welcomed by those in the ruling party particularly those in Saudi Arabia as the fledgling channel served not only as a competitor to the predominantly Saudi Arabian-owned media within the Middle East, but it also served as a challenger to the Saud Family. According to Pintak: "*Al Jazeera* gave the emir (of Qatar) power to drive public opinion in directions the Saudis did not necessarily like. That is why, early on, Saudi Arabia banned *Al Jazeera* journalists from within its border and unofficially barred its advertising agencies, which dominated the Gulf, from buying commercials on *Al Jazeera*." [42]

Saudi Arabia was not alone in its disdain for the rising network or its underestimation of the channel's capacity to influence political action. When *Al-Jazeera's* coverage of the Second Intifada "sparked furor among several countries igniting pro-Palestinian demonstrations across the Middle East, the network broadcasted opinions from Arabs calling on their leaders to do more for the Palestinians." This decision angered several Arab governments, namely Egypt, who accused *Al Jazeera* of trying to incite violence." Mohammad Abdul Monem, a spokesman for ousted Egyptian President Hosni Mubarak, believed that *Al Jazeera* was subversive and that it was deliberately trying to destabilize Arab governments: "They are undermining us. They are undermining Egypt, undermining Saudi Arabia, undermining all the Arab countries. They are separating the Arab world. It's no good."[43] Mubarak himself once famously quipped after a surprise visit to the *Al Jazeera* television studios in Doha in January 2000: "All this trouble from a matchbox like this!"[44] Ironically, eleven years later, Mubarak's Government would be accused of attempting to "jam" the network's signal days after he ordered the shutdown of *Al Jazeera's* operations in the country and an Egyptian satellite cut its broadcast signal."[45] In spite of this, "the network broadcast live from Cairo's Tahrir Square throughout the 18 days of protest, despite its office being closed, journalists beaten and detained, and tapes and equipment confiscated and destroyed."[46] Mubarak's actions proved to have little impact and *Al Jazeera's* global audience numbers "rocketed" as live stream viewers watching the channel over the internet increased by 2,500 percent to 4 million, 1.6 million of them in the United States.[47] For *Al Jazeera* this along with its earlier coverage of represented a major turning point in terms of journalistic credibility and global potential. Other countries like Algeria, Bahrain and Iraq have also banned *Al Jazeera* reporters from its borders during various periods of time in the last 10 years.

Controversy comes to *Al Jazeera*

Although *Al Jazeera* has embraced controversial topics and commentary on its programming, it has not been immune from its own controversy namely allegations of Qatari ruling party influence and lack of true editorial independence. Since the majority of funding for *Al Jazeera* has come from the Qatari ruling family, most researchers and media professionals suspect there is some editorial influence and certainly there are "red lines" for reporting. According to Lawrence Pintak, one of the world's leading scholars in the media of the Middle East: "*Al Jazeera* may have set the tone for an aggressive new style of journalism in the Arab world, but at the end of the day it was still owned by a government. Its so called 'red lines' – the limits beyond which reporters venture at their own peril – included stories that might negatively impact on Qatari foreign policy." [48]

Al Jazeera's coverage of the "Arab Spring", continuing uprisings in Syria and elsewhere in the world are being carefully monitored for any perceived bias or political ideology, which would hamper *Al Jazeera's* credibility and violate its own editorial principles. Of concern are recent assertions that *Al Jazeera* may be advancing the political cause of the *Muslim Brotherhood*, one of the Arab world's most influential and largest Islamic movements. Professor Seib warns: "there is the growing perception within the Arab world – particularly among Arab moderates—that *Al Jazeera* is becoming more overt in advancing the *Muslim Brotherhood* agenda. I have spoken with numerous people from the Middle East who consider *Al Jazeera's* coverage of Syria and its limited coverage of Bahrain as evidence of a highly politicized news organization. It is important to note that this issue relates to *Al Jazeera-Arabic*, while *Al Jazeera-English* continues to be widely praised for its objective, comprehensive news gathering."[49]

Further to these concerns, U.S. allegations of manipulation of *Al Jazeera's* content for political ends also contradict Qatar's claim to support a free press and *Al Jazeera's* editorial independence. In a series of diplomatic cables from the U.S. embassy in Qatar that were publicly released by *WikiLeaks* as part of the 2010 diplomatic cables leak, senior U.S. diplomats stated: "*Al Jazeera*, the most watched satellite television station in the Middle East, is heavily subsidized by the Qatari government and has proved itself a useful tool for the station's political masters. The station's coverage of events in the Middle East is relatively free and open, though it refrains from criticizing Qatar and its government."[50] In another instance, U.S. officials alleged the Qatari government manipulates "*Al Jazeera* coverage to suit political interests" and is "using *Al Jazeera* as a bargaining chip in foreign policy negotiations by adapting its coverage to suit other foreign leaders and offering to cease critical transmissions in exchange for major concessions."[51] Other critics have pointed to instances where *Al Jazeera* has "pulled its punches" as evidence of its political interference. "One American diplomatic cable alluded to improving relations between Qatar and Saudi Arabia were because of "toned down criticism of the Saudi royal family on *Al Jazeera*", while another suggested *Al Jazeera* could be used "as a bargaining tool to repair relationships with other countries, particularly those soured by *Al Jazeera's* broadcasts, including the United States" over the next three years."[52] In one dispatch, former U.S. ambassador to Qatar, Joseph LeBaron, suggested: "*Al Jazeera's* ability to influence public opinion throughout the region is a substantial source of leverage for Qatar, one which it is unlikely to relinquish." [53]

Despite repeated denials from senior officials at *Al Jazeera* of Qatar's influence, there is some recent evidence among *Al Jazeera* correspondents demonstrating a growing dissatisfaction with undue influence and lack of editorial objectivity. With the resignation of *Al Jazeera- Arabic's* Beirut correspondent, Ali Hashem, in March 2012 it drew attention to a growing concern of Qatari Government influence on *Al Jazeera* news coverage in Syria and Bahrain and further reinforced other's growing concerns. "Hashem's resignation came weeks after pro-Assad hackers leaked emails that revealed the dismay among *Al Jazeera*'s staff over its "biased and unprofessional" coverage of the Syrian uprising."[54] Additionally, the reporter believed *Al Jazeera* was not providing adequate coverage of the uprisings in Bahrain, a matter that several other *Al Jazeera* reporters noted as well. One source added: "In Bahrain, we were seeing pictures of a people being butchered by the 'Gulf's oppression machine', and for *Al Jazeera*, silence was the name of the game."[55] Another similar incident occurred in September 2012, when several *Al Jazeera-English* journalists protested the orders of their news director to edit a United Nations report in order to focus more closely on the Qatar emir's comments concerning Syria. These incidents, coupled with the resignation of the previous *Al Jazeera* Director General, Wadah Khanfar, have caused some to speculate the Qatari Government is attempting to exert even greater influence over the *Al Jazeera* programming and editorial positions.[56] Al Antsey, the managing director of

Al Jazeera-English denies any Qatari or governmental influence: "There's been no interaction from Qatar whatsoever. In Egypt we were on the ground very quickly, with force, in the first minutes and hours, with total editorial independence. Editorially, the Qatari government is completely hands-off."[57]

Although there is ample evidence on both sides of the discussion of *Al Jazeera's* editorial independence and Qatari influence, most experts agree that *Al Jazeera* is not unlike other media outlets in their editorial decisions. David Roberts, a researcher at Durham University in the United Kingdom offered: "I think *Al Jazeera* itself conducts self-censorship to ensure no red lines are crossed. But in general, the Qatari government is not cherry-picking stories or censoring. They let them run with any story they want, up to a certain point."[58]

***Al Jazeera* Bias**

Al Jazeera has not only generated a great deal of controversy for its editorial positions and decisions, it has also often been accused of bias. At one point or another, *Al Jazeera* has been described as "a Zionist agent," "an American agent," "an anti-Semitic station," "a bin Laden station," and "anti-American."[59] However, during an interview with *CNN* focused on the Arab Spring, Al Antsey fervently denied any existence of bias: "We are categorically anti-nothing, and pro-nothing. Our job is journalistic, to cover the facts on the ground and cover the whole story."[60] In spite of Antsey's claims, the allegations continue to detract from *Al Jazeera's* credibility and appeal to a broader audience.

One of the most cited examples of bias is *Al Jazeera's* perceived anti--Israel Bias, a label which has been difficult for the network to remove. In spite of *Al Jazeera's* groundbreaking decision to allow Israeli officials the opportunity to participate on several of their programs, a practice which was a historical first for any Arabic news network at that time, the network continues to be hampered by its perceived bias towards Israel and pro-Palestinian position. Author and historian, Hugh Miles offered: "Until *Al Jazeera* arrived, most Arabs had never even heard an Israeli's voice...The network covers Israeli affairs extensively and is widely watched in Israel. In fact, *Al Jazeera* gives more airtime to Israeli issues than any other channel outside Israel itself."[61] And even though Israel has accused *Al Jazeera* of bias, there have been some instances where *Al Jazeera's* news coverage has actually served to benefit Israel. Miles shared: "When Israel invaded Jenin in the spring of 2002, *Al Jazeera's* exclusive television reports from within the besieged city thoroughly dispelled rumors of a "massacre," leading to a U.N. special investigating committee appointed by the secretary-general being unceremoniously disbanded."[62]

The root of some of the anti-Israel assertions may stem from *Al Jazeera*'s reporting from the Second Intifada, where it described Palestinian suicide bombers as "martyrs", a term many would argue crossed the line of objective journalism.[63] Israel's common practice was to label suicide bombers as "homicide bombers", while most international and Western press outlets used the term "suicide bomber". The dramatic difference between how the majority of the international press labeled these individuals and how *Al Jazeera* portrayed them sparked the initial debate of *Al Jazeera's* journalistic objectivity and reporting. *Al Jazeera's* perceived lack of objectivity may in fact be linked to the proximity of its correspondents to the conflict. Unlike many Western news agencies, who traditionally manage news coverage of global events and crises with rotating personnel and regional bureaus, *Al Jazeera* prides itself on reporting from the ground level and with citizen journalists. In some cases, it becomes especially difficult to report without bias as in the case of Walid Al Omary, *Al Jazeera's* reporter in the West Bank city of Ramallah. Al Omary offered his explanation for perceived reporting bias: “To be objective in this area is not easy because we live here. We are part of the people here. And this situation belongs to us also, and we have our opinions.” [64] Many other Arab viewers feel similarly and are quick to point out television networks like *CNN* carry a heavy dose of bias towards Arabs and blatantly favor American foreign policy. As an example, these critics are quick to point out the U.S. media's lack of use of the term “assassination” when describing Israel's actions against Palestinian faction leaders. The decision to use “targeted killings” as an alternative phrase helps to fuel conspiracy and support allegations of pro-Israeli bias in Western-based media. [65]

As to the network's conveyance of an anti-American or anti-Western bias, there is considerable debate but no real substantive research to prove the assertions other than anecdotal evidence or observation. Hugh Miles offered: “During the war in Iraq, *Al Jazeera's* tone was notably sympathetic to the Iraqis and hostile toward the Americans. Similarly in Afghanistan, the Taliban was often presented as the noble underdog and America as the vengeful, colonial aggressor. A general cynicism about Arab regimes allied to America is detectable, and though *Al Jazeera* has employees from many religions, the network is clearly sympathetic toward the Palestinians. This bias in no way invalidates the network's news. Knowing it is scrutinized more rigorously than any other news channel in the world; *Al Jazeera* is fastidious in presenting all sides of a story." Dr. Eric Nisbet, Arab media expert at Ohio State University, also asserts there may be some bias in *Al Jazeera's* reporting. In reference to the Arabic channel of *Al Jazeera* he offered, "There are definitely some biases in that they are an Arabic channel for Arab audiences." But he also urged, "We as a country need to know what other people think of us. If we really want to make informed decisions about foreign policy and about the opportunities and challenges we face overseas, we need to hear that perspective. *Al Jazeera* provides a very non-American window on the world that we need to be looking through."[66] Sharon Waxman, the Vice President for Public Policy and Advocacy and Director of the Washington office of the International Rescue Committee offered: "The innovative nature of *Al Jazeera*, combined with its clear political point of view, creates a strange paradox. The network represents a quantum leap forward for unfettered journalism in the Arab world, yet it takes an approach that by Western standards would be considered lacking in basic fairness and balance. Still, by media standards in the Middle East -- where rumors about the United States poisoning relief packages in Afghanistan are printed in the paper, where newspapers whipped up a frenzy over the sale of leather belts that supposedly sapped male potency -- *Al Jazeera* is a model of fact-based reporting."[67]

The presence of bias by *Al Jazeera* in its reporting may actually be similar to the assertions of bias in the U.S.-based media, who tend to be more liberal or "left of center" in their editorial positions and reporting according to author and professor Tim Groseclose. He asserts in his research findings: "consistent with survey results that showed the personal views of journalists (U.S.) overwhelmingly lean left, most outlets were indeed left of center."[68] Yet even if Groseclose's observations are correct, most Americans would agree that the U.S. based news outlets are instrumental in maintaining accountability of the government, and vital in providing the world with an American perspective and opinion no matter how biased they may be. Additionally, just as the U.S. media has reflected the views and opinions of the American public following 9/11, *Al Jazeera* may also be accused of reflecting the same bias as its predominantly Arab and Muslim audiences. Interestingly, there is some evidence that suggests *Al Jazeera* and its channels may actually be a victim of American bias. In a recent study, researchers at the University of Michigan found "a substantial prejudice against *Al Jazeera-English* among segments of the American public."[69] This prejudice against *Al Jazeera-English* seemed to be highly correlated with conservative political ideology and anti-Arab sentiments.[70]

While most *Al Jazeera* viewers dismiss allegations that the channel is pro- Al Qaeda or serves as a mouthpiece for its followers, many say *Al Jazeera* can at times appear to be sympathetic to extremist groups such as Hamas, which won the Palestinian elections in 2006 over the more secular, Fatah. These assertions may stem from *Al Jazeera's* decision to publish "leaked documents revealing that the Fatah-led Palestinian Authority had offered multiple concessions to Israel in peace talks. The revelations, which *Al Jazeera* shared with Britain's Guardian newspaper, made the Palestinian Authority and Fatah look weak and led to the resignation of Chief Palestinian negotiator Saeb Erekat, who has accused *Al Jazeera* trying to bring down the Palestinian Authority."[71] Another potential reason for these allegations may be Al

Qaeda's repeated sharing of videos and news information with *Al Jazeera* bureaus and correspondents. It was *Al Jazeera* that decided to show the first televised broadcast of a ninety-minute discussion with Osama bin Laden to a mass Arab audience in June 1999.[72] Since that decision, the network, bin Laden, and Al Qaeda have been inextricably linked. As evidenced by their repeated emphasis on providing *Al Jazeera* with video and audio-taped messages from its leaders during the period of 2001-2006, it is clear Al Qaeda and other extremist organizations recognized *Al Jazeera's* unique ability to extend considerable influence into the broader Muslim community and reach their target audience. [73] Recognizing who *Al Jazeera*'s target audience is (20-25 year old Muslim males) and *Al Jazeera's* universal appeal to that group, it is not difficult to understand why Al Qaeda and others would attempt to leverage *Al Jazeera* as a platform for their rhetoric and recruiting propaganda. However, Marc Lynch, suggested their strategy to try and use *Al Jazeera* as a platform for their ideology may have actually backfired: "*Al Jazeera* and other satellite television stations have unleashed powerful counter-forces and political competitors into a once-vacant arena. Indeed, the migration of the jihad onto the Internet associated with Abu Musab al-Zarqawi's rise to prominence directly responds to his dismay with *Al Jazeera's* challenge to the jihad."[74]

Given the lack of comprehensive study proving the existence of biased reporting by *Al Jazeera* or its affiliated channels, there appears to be little evidence to support many of the assertions and allegations regarding bias. However, *Al Jazeera's* increasing ability to serve as a powerful and influential communicator to a global audience necessitates further study and engagement by the world's leaders.

II. *Al Jazeera* and its Rocky Relationship with the United States

Although *Al Jazeera* has faced intense scrutiny and opposition from the authoritarian regimes in power throughout the Middle East, perhaps the largest critique and the loudest critic of *Al Jazeera* has come from the one country that most espouses freedom of the press, the United States. Although initially hailed by the United States and its allies for its example of press freedom in the Arab world, *Al Jazeera* found itself under intense American scrutiny for its airing of the post 9/11 video tapes of bin Laden. Former U.S. Secretary of Defense Donald Rumsfeld once described the network's reporting as "vicious, inaccurate and inexcusable" during a news conference in April 2004. [75] Other organizations like Accuracy in Media (AIM), have called it "a mouthpiece of Al Qaeda propaganda".[76] A careful examination of the history of the relationship between the U.S. Government and *Al Jazeera* can serve as a foundation for greater understanding and perhaps as a catalyst for greater engagement.

November 1996-September 2001: Implicit Approval and Heightened Awareness

Prior to September 2001, the relationship between *Al Jazeera* and the United States could best be described as a period of implicit approval and heightened awareness of the network's importance to democracy in the Arab world. With its first broadcast in November 1996, *Al Jazeera* was welcomed by the U.S. and its allies as a model for independent reporting in an area of the world that was overwhelmingly adversarial to press freedom. Breaking the mold and many taboos of traditional Arab journalism, *Al Jazeera* was hailed as a "beacon of light" by an official in the Clinton White House and praised by Israeli leadership as well for its willingness to offer them opportunities for interviews and opinions on multiple programs.[77] Beyond government officials, a 1997 survey published in Al-Sharq, a Qatari newspaper found that 79% of Washington, DC residents “strongly supported” *Al Jazeera* and its programming.[78] The United States Information Agency also enjoyed a positive working relationship with *Al Jazeera* as evidenced by its decision to share a taped message from President Clinton addressed to the Arab world on American policy towards Iraq in February 1998. *Al Jazeera* was one of only two media outlets to receive the advance copy of the taped message and chose to broadcast the message in its entirety. “Although few commentators agreed with the U.S. position, there was recognition of the gesture the President had made in addressing the people of the Middle East.”[79] Similarly, even though *Al Jazeera’s* 1998 coverage was critical of the U.S. led “Desert Fox” operation, a military effort intended to "degrade" Iraq's ability to manufacture and use weapons of mass destruction, it was still highly regarded in both the West and the Middle East.[80] Moreover, the general opinion of *Al Jazeera* among the U.S. Government and its employees prior to the fall of 2001 could be summed up in the following quote by a U.S. State Department employee: “We recognize it [*Al Jazeera*] as a powerful voice with a wide viewership in the Arab world.”[81]

However, following the events of September 11, 2001, *Al Jazeera’s* wide ranging programming, editorial decisions, and its opinionated presenters and guests caused many to begin to question *Al Jazeera’s* role and responsibility as an independent media source during times of global crisis and war. The situation began to deteriorate upon *Al Jazeera’s* decision to read a statement reportedly authored by bin Laden on the air only days after the attacks in America. Although bin Laden denied any involvement with the attacks in the video, where he stated "I stress that I have not carried out this act, which appears to have been carried out by individuals with their own motivation", U.S. officials were already suspicious of bin Laden's complicity based on earlier Israeli intelligence warnings.[82] While *Al Jazeera*'s decision to air this statement brought increased international ratings and attention, it also brought increased suspicion by the United States and its citizens. Moreover, its unique access to bin Laden also led to mounting public scrutiny especially from the U.S. Government and its allies. As the only Arab news outlet with a functional bureau in Kabul, Afghanistan, *Al Jazeera* became the network of choice for bin Laden and his supporters to continue to propagate their ideologies through statements, video-taped messages and images. To some, *Al Jazeera* simply provided bin Laden and his supporters with a "pipeline to the Arab and Muslim people as he launched his military and propaganda assault on the U.S."[83] *Al Jazeera's* unique access also allowed the network to broadcast the only video pictures of Afghan demonstrators attacking and setting fire to the US Embassy in Kabul on September 26th. This broadcast further infuriated the American leadership and increased speculation concerning the network's amicable association with the Taliban and bin Laden.[84]

October 2001-October 2006: Intensified Animosity and Acrimony

Following the commencement of the bombing in Afghanistan, *Al Jazeera's* relationship with the U.S. and its senior leadership dramatically transformed from approval to adversarial. The seeds for this dramatic shift may have actually been sown prior to the commencement of the Afghanistan Campaign. In a meeting on October 4,

2001, only days prior to the commencement of the air attacks into Afghanistan, Qatari's ruler Sheikh Hamad bin Khalifa al Thani met with then Secretary of State Colin Powell. It was reported that *Al Jazeera* was the topic of discussion and the emir "was defensive about the issue and countered that he did not feel *Al Jazeera* was any more inflammatory than any other Arab media outlet."[85] Four days later, *Al Jazeera* would broadcast a statement by bin Laden challenging America and its presence in the Middle East. In a recorded video message broadcast after the strikes, bin Laden praised the September 11 attacks in the United States and said "a group of Muslims" was responsible. He continued by stating: "America has been hit by Allah at its most vulnerable point, destroying, thank God, its most prestigious buildings."[86] This decision caused even greater angst, prompting Powell's assertion that *Al Jazeera* is providing "time and attention to some very vitriolic, irresponsible kinds of statements." [87] *Al Jazeera* vehemently defended its decisions to air the tape as indicated by the statements of its news editor at that time, Ahmed Sheikh. He claimed that any news channel considered to be objective would have aired the statements released by bin Laden. "Osama bin Laden, like it or not, is a party to this present crisis... If we said that we were not going to allow him the air time, then we would have lost our integrity and objectivity and our coverage of the story would have become unbalanced."[88]

From *Al Jazeera's* perspective the relationship was also rapidly deteriorating. Following the destruction of its Kabul news bureau on November 13, 2001 by a U.S. missile, *Al Jazeera* suspected this was a deliberate attack because of *Al Jazeera's* access and reporting of the conflict in Afghanistan. Even though there were no casualties, *Al Jazeera's* managing director at that time; Mohammed Jasim al-Ali voiced his displeasure in an interview with the *BBC* following the bombing. He claimed: "This office has been known by everybody, the American airplanes know the location of the office, they know we are broadcasting from there."[89] The seeds of mistrust in Afghanistan grew even more when one of *Al Jazeera's* reporters, Sami Al Hajj, was arrested by Pakistani Security Forces as a suspected Al Qaeda operative in December 2001. Despite *Al Jazeera's* assertions of his innocence and pleas for his release, Al Haj would be detained for nearly six and a half years at the U.S. Detention Facility in Guantanamo Bay, Cuba.[90]

With the invasion of Iraq in March 2003, the chasm of mistrust between *Al Jazeera* and the U.S. continued to widen following its decision to broadcast images of dead and captured American Soldiers in Iraq during the early stages of the invasion. On March 22, 2003, *Al Jazeera* broadcasted video footage of five captured American Soldiers from the 507th Maintenance Company answering questions from their Iraqi captors. According to sources, there appeared to be "at least four dead bodies in U.S. uniforms also visible in the broadcasts, some with apparent gunshot wounds to the head."[91] This decision angered many Americans namely, the U.S. military and political leadership "for broadcasting the images to much of the Arab world."[92] Other U.S. officials accused *Al Jazeera* of supporting Iraqi propaganda and for violating international rules on handling of prisoners of war. In his testimony to the House Armed Service Committee on April 4, 2003, W. Hays Parks, special assistant to the Judge Advocate General of the Army, publicly stated: "Iraqi Television and *Al Jazeera* have aired a tape of U.S. Soldiers answering questions in humiliating and insulting circumstances designed to make them objects of public curiosity, in violation of the

Geneva Convention."[93] *Al Jazeera* defended its decision to air the images of the dead American Soldiers by saying "they had to air the pictures so that Americans can make up their own minds about the Iraq War."[94]

The animosity from the political and military leadership for *Al Jazeera* was also growing in other areas of the United States namely, New York City and Wall Street. A day after the broadcast of the American POW's, *Al Jazeera's* reporters were banned from the *New York Stock Exchange (NYSE)*. Citing "overcrowding on the exchange floor" and "security reasons", the exchange decided to revoke *Al Jazeera's* press credentials and access to the exchange.[95] Although the *NYSE* denied the revocation had anything to do with *Al Jazeera's* coverage of the Iraq War, Robert Zito, the exchange's executive vice president for communications, said that while crowding was a consideration, "I think the stuff over the weekend (referring to *Al Jazeera's* broadcast of images of American prisoners and dead soldiers), as I'm looking at where our priorities should be, led me to believe that if I was trying to accommodate responsible news organizations, I couldn't include *Al Jazeera* in that group."[96] Although the *NYSE* ban of *Al Jazeera* would be reversed months later, its initial decision met with mixed response in America, namely from academics and experts in journalism such as Robert M. Steele, an expert in journalism ethics at the Poynter Institute, who "was concerned that the expulsion of working journalists could create a bad precedent, and lead to retaliation against American journalists. He was also struck, by the incident's many ironies: Expelling reporters for an Arab network during a war that is in part about exporting American freedoms to Iraq. Punishing *Al Jazeera*, which is widely recognized as one of the most influential news organizations in the Arab world -- where the United States is struggling to influence public opinion."[97] *Al Jazeera* was also denied access to the *Nasdaq* Stock Market later that same week due to its broadcasting of the images of the American prisoners. Unlike the *NYSE*, the *Nasdaq* leadership clearly articulated the rationale for their decision as indicated by the statement of Nasdaq spokesman Scott Peterson: "In light of *Al Jazeera*'s recent conduct during the war, in which they have broadcast footage of U.S. POWs in alleged violation of the Geneva Convention, they are not welcome to broadcast from our facility at this time."[98] In addition to the bans on Wall Street, *Akamai Technologies*, a Cambridge, Massachusetts-based internet developer "cancelled a contract to provide web services for *Al Jazeera's* new English language website."[99] *Al Jazeera's* reservations and suspicions of the U.S. Government were not just limited to what was occurring in the United States.

The rising tide of animosity between *Al Jazeera* and the United States Government reached a new zenith in the midst of the war in Iraq first, with the U.S. military's artillery shelling of a hotel in Basra on April 2, 2003, where *Al Jazeera's* correspondents were residing [100]and second, when *Al Jazeera's* Baghdad news bureau was struck by a U.S. missile a few days later in a similar manner to their bureau in Kabul.[101] Although there were no casualties in the first of these two incidents, one of *Al Jazeera's* reporters in Basra asserted the Pentagon was fully informed of their location: "Al-Jazeera had officially advised the Pentagon of all relevant details pertaining to its reporters covering the war on Iraq, as stipulated by relevant international practice and conventions governing reporting wars. The details included official HQs of all its reporters in Basra, Mosul and Baghdad."[102] In the second incident, there were casualties including the death of Tarek Ayoub, a Jordanian *Al Jazeera* reporter.

Although the U.S. military denied the allegation, *Al Jazeera's* chief editor at that time, Ibrahim Hilal said the "U.S. military has long known the map coordinates and street number of his network's office. Witnesses saw the plane fly over twice before dropping the bombs. Our office is in a residential area, and even the Pentagon knows its location."[103] Ayoub's widow, now an outspoken critic of the U.S. and its military, also claimed the Pentagon knew of the *Al Jazeera* bureau's location far in advance of the offensive campaign to take Baghdad. In an editorial for the British-based newspaper *The Guardian,* she stated: *Al Jazeera* had "given the precise location of the station's Baghdad office to the Pentagon three months before the war. My husband and the others were killed in broad daylight, in locations known to the Pentagon as media sites."[104] She would also later initiate a $30 million lawsuit against the Bush administration alleging they were responsible for the wrongful death of her husband in the bombing incident.[105]

Meanwhile, America's disdain for *Al Jazeera* continued to spread beyond Washington, DC and New York City, this time manifesting itself in Boston, the site of the 2004 Democratic National Convention. On July 19, 2004, *Al Jazeera* staff members discovered a banner with *Al Jazeera's* name and logo on it had mysteriously disappeared from where it was being displayed in front of its broadcasting location inside the venue. Even though the network had received advance approval for displaying its sign, its sign was removed because it would have been seen in every wide-angle cutaway shot to the audience. According to *Al Jazeera's* Washington, DC bureau manager, Stephanie Thomas, "It was removed, even though no other banners in the same sightline were taken down."[106] Although the sign was eventually located some

15 miles away from the convention site, the incident revealed the declining public opinion and acceptance of *Al Jazeera* on American soil. Adding fuel to the fire, *Al Jazeera* also became victim to a homespun American hoax later that same month, when it aired a video of an American appearing to be being beheaded on July 31.[107] Although the video's maker, Benjamin Vanderford admitted to staging the video to attract attention, *Al Jazeera* was harshly criticized for its decision to air the images. Although an obvious hoax, the network's displaying of these images has perpetuated one of the biggest fallacies about the network since its inception and has proven to be one of the hardest stigmas to remove especially in America; an image of Al Qaeda sanctioned beheadings being proliferated on *Al Jazeera's* airwaves.[108]

Al Jazeera was also struggling to report on the War in Iraq as it faced increased scrutiny and suspensions from the interim Iraqi Government due to its alleged incitement of violence against Iraqi and American officials and troops. For the second time in a year, Iraqi officials chose to suspend *Al Jazeera's* news bureau from reporting in Iraq blaming *Al Jazeera's* coverage of terror attacks and kidnappings for increased levels of violence in the late summer of 2004. According to Iraqi Interior Minister Falah al-Naqib, "They have encouraged the criminals and the gangsters to increase their activities in the country, which has suffered a lot."[109] *Al Jazeera* publicly condemned the decision as Hafez Al-Mirazi, *Al-Jazeera's* Washington bureau chief stated: "It's really regrettable that a government that was installed in power mainly to give and provide a model for democracy and peace is just mimicking other authoritarian regimes."[110] In response to the closing, then Secretary of Defense Rumsfeld offered: "They have persuaded an enormous fraction of the people that we're there as an occupying force, which is a lie, that we are randomly killing innocent civilians, which is a lie."[111] The Government of Iraq would later extend the ban on *Al Jazeera* from reporting in Iraq citing *Al Jazeera's* failure to comply with the requirements of the original ban.[112] The ban on its reporters would remain in effect until March 2007, when Iraqi Prime Minister Nouri al Maliki agreed to allow its reporters back into the country on a trial basis due in large part to the personal intervention by Multi-National Force Iraq Commander General David Petraeus and then, Major General William B. Caldwell, IV, the coalition spokesman in Iraq at that time.[113] Unfortunately, the *Al Jazeera* bureau in Baghdad would not be reopened until March 2011, nearly seven years after its original closure.[114]

One of the most controversial topics related to the relationship between *Al Jazeera* and the United States involved the alleged discussion between former President George W. Bush and then Prime Minister Tony Blair of the United Kingdom, where the two senior leaders reportedly discussed plans to bomb *Al Jazeera's* headquarters in Doha, Qatar. Publicly called "The *Al Jazeera* bombing memo", the five-page document was published in a British tabloid, *The Mirror* on November 22, 2005. The memorandum was touted to be a record of a meeting between the two senior leaders, which occurred on April 16, 2004 during the conduct of the assault on the Iraqi city of Fallujah, also called Operation Vigilant Resolve. Following the publication of the report, the White House dismissed the allegations as "outlandish", but *Al Jazeera* demanded the British government to confirm or deny the report.[115] Although neither confirming nor denying the report, the British government curiously held two men accountable for releasing the information to the public under Britain's "Official Secrets Act of 1989."[116] On May 10, 2007, David Keogh, a civil servant at the Cabinet Office of the United Kingdom, “was found guilty on two counts of making a "damaging disclosure" by revealing the memo and was sentenced to 6 months in jail. He was also ordered to pay £5000 in costs to the prosecution. The other individual, Leo O'Connor, a research assistant was sentenced to 3 months in jail.”[117] Although the memo still remains a mystery for all involved parties, it continues to serve as fuel for further conspiracy theories and one of several unresolved concerns for many of *Al Jazeera's* most senior employees. While the relationship with America continued to erode, some believe the animosity from the Bush administration was actually serving to fuel *Al Jazeera's* growing popularity across the globe, in particular in other English-speaking nations.[118]

The following is an illustrative timeline of key events between the U.S. Government and *Al Jazeera* during the period September 2001-November 2006 with the official start up of *Al Jazeera- English*. The timeline includes information obtained from multiple sources including the *Pew Research Center's Project for Excellence in Journalism*, *Al Jazeera*, and the *Committee to Protect Journalists*.[119]

Date	Incident/Event
September 16, 2001	*Al Jazeera* reads a statement on the air reportedly provided to them by Osama bin Laden.
September 26, 2001	*Al Jazeera* broadcasts video images of Afghan demonstrators attacking and setting fire to the US Embassy in Kabul.
October 3, 2001	U.S. Secretary of State Colin Powell meets with Sheikh Hamad bin Khalifa al-Thani, the Qatari emir expressing concern about *Al Jazeera*.
October 7, 2001	*Al Jazeera* broadcasts a statement by bin Laden after the US-led coalition begins military strikes against Afghanistan.
October 30, 2001	U.S. Secretary of Defense Donald Rumsfeld accuses the network of promoting Taliban propaganda.
November 3, 2001	*Al Jazeera* airs a second tape of bin Laden, which he

	accuses the West, the UN, and Israel, of pursuing a fundamentally religious war.
November 13, 2001	U.S. missiles strike *Al Jazeera*'s news bureau in Kabul, Afghanistan.
December 15, 2001	Sami Al Hajj, a Sudanese journalist working for *Al Jazeera* as a cameraman is arrested by the Pakistani Army while traveling to Afghanistan on a legitimate visa.
March 22, 2003	*Al Jazeera* broadcasts video footage of five American POWs and other dead U.S. Soldiers
March 24, 2003	The *New York Stock Exchange* bans *Al Jazeera* from its trading floor indefinitely, citing "security concerns" as the official reason.
April 2, 2003	U.S. military's shelling of a hotel in Basra, where *Al Jazeera* reporters were staying and reporting.
April 8, 2003	U.S. bombs hit *Al Jazeera's* office in Baghdad, killing reporter Tareq Ayyoub and wounding a cameraman.
September 23, 2003	The Iraqi interim government suspends *Al Jazeera* for a two-week period for its alleged support for violence against Iraqi Government officials and U.S. troops.
July 19, 2004	*Al Jazeera's* banner is removed from the Democratic National Convention in Boston.
July 31, 2004	*Al Jazeera* airs a hoaxed tape of an American being beheaded.
August 7, 2004	The Iraqi interim government shuts down the Baghdad office of *Al Jazeera* for one month, citing national security concerns.
November 22, 2005	The British tabloid, the Daily Mirror, publishes a story claiming it had obtained a leaked memo from someone in Prime Minister Tony Blair's cabinet saying that President George Bush had considered bombing *Al Jazeera's* Doha headquarters in April 2004.
July 11, 2006	Dima Ayyoub, the widow of the *Al Jazeera* reporter who was killed in the 2003 bombing of the Baghdad bureau, sues the Bush administration for $30 million for the death of her husband.
November 15, 2006	*Al Jazeera-English* first broadcast

November 2006-November 2010: Improved Acceptance and Access

With the official launch of *Al Jazeera-English* on November 15, 2006, it signaled an opportunity for both sides to renew dialogue and provided a platform for the U.S. Government to engage in on camera interviews without requiring the use of translators. This period of time seemed to be marked by a graduated level of acceptance by the U.S. and its leaders of *Al Jazeera* and its rising influence as a global news leader as evidenced by the increased number of interviews of U.S. leaders following the launch of *Al Jazeera-English*. Not surprisingly the gradual warming coincided with the departure of one of *Al Jazeera*'s most outspoken critics, Donald Rumsfeld, who retired in December 2006 and was replaced by Robert Gates, a leader who would later appear in multiple *Al Jazeera* interviews over his tenure as the U.S. Secretary of Defense. This period of growing acceptance also coincided with the Bush administration and its public diplomacy efforts to reach a larger international audience in particular citizens within the Middle East.

One of these initiatives included routine outreach and participation on *Al Jazeera* programs by both U.S. State Department and officials in the U.S. DoD as they travelled to and from Doha along with assigning spokespeople in Dubai, UAE and Doha to coordinate and communicate with the various Arab media outlets, namely *Al Jazeera*. *Al Jazeera's* senior leadership embraced the outreach efforts and greater access to U.S. spokesperson suggesting they were willing to move beyond many of the previous misgivings in the relationship. In a 2007 *PBS Frontline* interview with then Director General for *Al Jazeera* Wadah Khanfar, the presenter asked Khanfar if this outreach was helpful for the network. Khanfar's response suggested a willingness to embrace better participation by the U.S. in the dialogue with *Al Jazeera*. He stated: "Actually, it is always helpful for me as a network. Always we would like to get more opinions about reality in order to give fair and balanced coverage. That's definitely true...But definitely from the network perspective, from a journalistic perspective, the more access you have to people who are decision makers or stakeholders is important."[120]

Al Jazeera-English also sought to establish better relations with the U.S. and its allies through the hiring of numerous correspondents who had significant experience in western-style journalism and credibility with many of the senior U.S. officials in both the State Department and the DoD. Among the newcomers, David Frost, a former *BBC* and *NBC* program host enjoyed a long-standing reputation as an unbiased and well informed media personality in both the United Kingdom and the United States. Known for his tough and direct series of interviews of British prime ministers and U.S. presidents including former U.S. President, Richard Nixon in 1977, Frost's hiring represented a dramatic improvement in *Al Jazeera's* image and reputation as a global news provider. By presenting a live weekly hour-long current affairs program, "Frost Over the World", the program has featured interviewees such as Tony Blair, Benazir Bhutto and President Daniel Ortega of Nicaragua.[121]

Another recruit to *Al Jazeera-English* was Josh Rushing, a former U.S. Marine Corps officer and spokesman for General Tommy Franks the former Commander of the United States Central Command (USCENTCOM). In his capacity as a public affairs officer, Rushing had gained notoriety for his participation in a 2004 documentary called

"Control Room" that recounted *Al Jazeera's* interactions with the USCENTCOM headquarters during the early phases of the Iraq War. In the film, Rushing is portrayed as a "Marine with a conscience" as he wrestles with what he believes and the images he sees on *Al Jazeera*.[122] After serving for 14 years, Rushing would later resign his commission from the Marine Corps and accept a position with *Al Jazeera-English* as an international correspondent. Given Rushing's background, knowledge, experience, and working relationships with both *Al Jazeera* and the U.S. military, he was an ideal candidate to help pursue greater engagement with the America and its senior leadership. Unfortunately, by his own account the challenges to doing this have been significant. He added: "The outrage over *Al Jazeera* in the United States often seems to boil down to the fact that they allow airtime to perspectives that are not deemed politically correct according to mainstream American standards."[123] In addition to added credibility for the network, both Frost and Rushing helped pave the way for *Al Jazeera* to gain access to some of America's top senior leaders, a process that would help fuel *Al Jazeera*'s growing acceptance within America in the following years.

With the change in U.S. presidential leadership in January 2009, the relationship between the two institutions continued to improve. Although President Obama chose to grant *Al Jazeera's* chief Arabic news rival, *Al Arabiya* an exclusive interview, the decision to choose an Arabic news channel as the new president's first formal television interview was a significant divergence from the previous administration. As part of the President's remarks during the interview, he highlighted his administration's desire to adopt a more extensive and regional approach in its relationship with the Muslim world. He stated: "we are ready to initiate a new partnership based on mutual respect and mutual interest," while also noting that "only then can progress be achieved."[124] The President's decision to choose an Arabic network coupled with his remarks, marked renewed optimism within most Middle Eastern-based news outlets of better relations with the U.S. Government and its senior leadership, chief among them was *Al Jazeera*.

December 2010-Present: Increased Approval and Appreciation

Although the remainder of 2009 and all of 2010 were marked by improving relations with *Al Jazeera*, it was not until the beginnings of the Arab Spring uprisings, first in Tunisia and Algeria in December 2010 followed by Egypt, Libya and Yemen in 2012 that *Al Jazeera* would not only gain wide-spread acceptance within the international community, but also significant approval and admiration by the United States and many of its senior leaders. Even as Americans like Cliff Kincaid, the director of the AIM Center for Investigative Journalism, who was urging American cable companies to not air *Al Jazeera* programming[125] and others like Pamela Geller , an American blogger, author, political activist, and commentator who has called *Al Jazeera* the "leading terrorist propaganda organization in the world,"[126] *Al Jazeera* continued to emerge as an influential and adaptive global news provider in the eyes of many in the United States Government as scenes unfolded from the Middle East in the early months of 2011.

Al Jazeera's coverage of these events in the Middle East seemed to be the tipping point in its widespread acceptance and approval among American senior leaders and politicians. It also served as a catalyst for greater engagement between the network and the United States, which seemed to be long overdue in the eyes of many in the public sphere when in January 2011; it was *Al Jazeera* that provided the world with some of the first images of the Arab Spring. The images and coverage prompted then-Secretary of State, Hillary Clinton to single out *Al Jazeera* for its coverage of the events in the Middle East as she spoke before the Senate Foreign Relations Committee in March 2011. She alluded to the fact that the U.S. is losing the "information war" in the world and highlighted how other countries and global news media were "making inroads" into places like the Middle East better than the United States. One of the reasons she cited for this change was the quality of channels like *Al Jazeera*. The channel, she said, was "changing peoples' minds and attitudes. And like it or hate it, it is really effective." She also added: "In fact viewership of *Al Jazeera* is going up in the United States because it's real news. You may not agree with it, but you feel like you're getting real news around the clock instead of a million commercials and, you know, arguments between talking heads and the kind of stuff that we do on our news which, you know, is not particularly informative to us, let alone foreigners."[127] Clinton had also visited *Al Jazeera's* Doha headquarters while visiting Qatar in February 2010 to "further dialogue with *Al Jazeera*" and to conduct a taped interview.[128] Clinton's staff also heaped praise on *Al Jazeera* and further validated a shift in approval of the network by the United States. According to Dana Shell Smith, the State Department's Principal Deputy Assistant Secretary for Public Affairs, who speaks Arabic and has frequently conducted interviews on the channel. "They are a really important media entity, and we have a really great relationship with them. This administration has empowered those of us who actually do the communicating to be in a close relationship with *Al-Jazeera*. They understand that the relationship can't consist of complaining to each other about the differences we have."[129] Although not directly endorsing the network, President Obama provided public comments that alluded to his approval of their efforts as well. He stated: "The emir of Qatar come by the Oval Office today, and he owns *Al-Jazeera* basically. Pretty influential guy. He is a big booster, big promoter of democracy all throughout the Middle East. Reform, reform, reform. You're seeing it on *Al-Jazeera*."[130]

The wellspring of approval for *Al Jazeera* even found its way into the Halls of Congress, where Senator John McCain, one of the most respected members of the U.S. Congress also publicly praised the efforts of *Al Jazeera* during a Washington, DC forum hosted by *Al Jazeera*. Lauding their coverage of the Tunisian uprising, McCain stated: "What *Al Jazeera* has done is achieved something that all of us I think want to achieve, particularly as we grow older, and that is to make a contribution that will last and will be brought to future generations that lie ahead of us. I want to assure you that these young people who were able to watch *Al Jazeera* and be inspired by the example of others is a remarkable achievement." McCain also highlighted the fact that he was the first U.S. senator to travel to *Al Jazeera*'s headquarters in Doha and sit for interviews.[131] McCain's comments at the forum were preceded by Senator Nancy Pelosi, who was as equally supportive of *Al Jazeera* in her remarks, where she congratulated *Al Jazeera* for its role in the Arab Spring.[132]

Author, Marc Lynch offered his assessment of the shift in the relationship between *Al Jazeera* and the U.S. "There has been a switch on the perception of *Al Jazeera-Arabic*, simply because right now, the U.S. and *Al Jazeera-Arabic* are more aligned in backing the democracy movements. It's not like *Al Jazeera* or the U.S. have changed that much. The issues have changed." Regardless of the cause for the shift the tide had turned at the highest levels of U.S. Government and politics. Even two of the most outspoken critics of *Al Jazeera*, Colin Powell and Donald Rumsfeld seemed to have a change of heart in their opinions of *Al Jazeera.* In a *Boston Globe* interview with Colin Powell's daughter in February 2011, she quoted her father as saying, "You should watch *Al Jazeera*. It's really in-depth coverage."[133] Powell would also later appear as a guest on *Al Jazeera* on the tenth anniversary of 9/11.[134] Rumsfeld equally lauded *Al Jazeera's* news coverage during an interview that aired in September 2011, where he stated: "Its audience has grown and it can be an important means of communication in the world, and I am delighted you are doing what you are doing."[135] This monumental shift in opinion from two of the most opinionated leaders in the prosecution of America's Global War on Terror, serves as perhaps the strongest evidence of the major shift that has occurred in the relationship between the United States Government and *Al Jazeera;* a relationship that appears to be continuously improving.

III. *Al Jazeera* and the U.S. Department of Defense

Much like the other institutions of the U.S. Government, the DoD's relationship with *Al Jazeera* has mirrored the pattern with *Al Jazeera* principally at the senior leadership levels.

Under the leadership of William Cohen, who was an active participant on *Al Jazeera* programming both while in his tenure as Secretary of Defense as well as after, the relationship was amicable even though U.S. policies were not always in agreement with the *Al Jazeera* editorial positions. Cohen's most notable appearance occurred in February 1998, when he participated in an interview at the *Al Jazeera* studio in Doha;

marking the first time a U.S. Secretary of Defense would be interviewed at the *Al Jazeera* studios.[136] Since Cohen's resignation from his position in January 2001, he has been a frequent guest on *Al Jazeera* programming including a December 2007 appearance with his wife on *Al Jazeera-English's* "The Riz Khan Show", where the couple discussed their experiences with racial and ethnic attitudes in the United States.[137] Cohen's tenure and the corresponding open engagement with *Al Jazeera* would come to an end in January 2001, with the arrival of Donald Rumsfeld.

Just as the world dramatically changed with the terrorist attacks of September 2011, the DoD's relationship with *Al Jazeera* under Rumsfeld's leadership did likewise. Given Rumsfeld public statements, such as calling the network's reporting "vicious, inaccurate and inexcusable"[138] and the unexplained U.S. military's missile strikes on both its Kabul and Baghdad news offices, *Al Jazeera*'s relationship with the Pentagon's top leadership took a dramatic turn for the worse. To be sure, the Pentagon was reaching out to *Al Jazeera* in the early part of 2003 as indicated by the participation of two senior civilians, Douglas Feith, the Under Secretary for Policy and Bryan Whitman, Deputy Assistant Secretary of Defense for Public Affairs, in separate interviews on *Al Jazeera* in January and April 2003, respectively. To his credit, Rumsfeld also did conduct a wide-ranging and non-combative interview with *Al Jazeera* prior to the commencement of the Iraq War, where he outlined the rationale for invading Iraq and the role the United States would play as part of a larger coalition.[139] However, Rumsfeld's opinion of the network seemed to sour shortly after the Iraq War began in the wake of *Al Jazeera's* decision to show American POW's. During an interview on *CBS*'s "Face the Nation", Rumsfeld demonstrated his disapproval of the network following the showing of the videos, where he stated: “And it seems to me that showing a few pictures on the screen, not knowing who they are and being communicated by *Al-Jazeera*, which is not a perfect instrument of communication in my view, obviously is part of Iraqi propaganda.” [140]

Rumsfeld’s further frustration with *Al Jazeera* would continue to surface in news briefings and interviews, where at one point he inferred the network’s journalists were working in collusion with insurgents in Iraq, allegations *Al Jazeera* vehemently denied. Calling the network “Johnny-on-the-spot”, he also asserted: "Sometimes journalists just happen to be there [at the scene]. But we know for a fact that other times the terrorists have told journalists - and I use the word inadvisably, quote unquote journalists - they've told journalists where they are going to be and what they're going to do. And the journalists have been there."[141] Rumsfeld’s public comments came at an extremely tense period of time for the U.S. military in Iraq as a mounting insurgency was claiming more and more American lives as the war moved into its second year. As equally frustrating for *Al Jazeera* was the Iraqi interim government’s decision to ban the network from reporting within Iraq by implementing a month-long ban that would later be extended indefinitely in September 2004. Claiming its reporting was backing "criminals and gangsters" by airing parts of videotapes from groups claiming to have seized or killed foreign hostages, the ban was suspected by many in *Al Jazeera* as the work of the U.S. military.[142] Although, the bureau would remain closed until March 2011, *Al Jazeera* reporters would eventually be able to return to the country in March 2007.

Interestingly, the hostility and opposition towards *Al Jazeera* that permeated throughout the Pentagon did not seem to match the feelings from the frontlines. In discussions with his former Marine colleagues, Josh Rushing recounted some of their comments to him concerning *Al Jazeera*: "I have received emails and phone calls from commanders in Iraq who have said, 'We think you're right about *Al Jazeera*. The military needs to work with them.' They want to engage the network through me but their hands have been tied."[143] To DoD's and USCENTCOM's credit, there was a pioneering effort undertaken within the United Arab Emirates and Qatar to reach out to the Arab press outlets and to provide each with greater access to DoD senior officials and military leaders. Much like the U.S. State Department had done in both Dubai and Doha respectively, USCENTCOM established a small media outreach team consisting of two U.S. military officers and a couple of civilian interpreters/translators. The team, headed by a U.S. Navy captain and a U.S. Army Reserve captain did yeoman's work in establishing improved relations with each of the Dubai and Abu Dhabi–based press outlets through their daily engagement and outreach to the various senior editors and producers of the Arab press.[144] The small team also travelled to Doha multiple times during the week to meet with *Al Jazeera's* senior officials and to conduct interviews, if needed. They also proved to be invaluable spokesmen and coordinators as news stories from Afghanistan and Iraq were breaking. Through the use of various communication means, they were able to rapidly respond to news queries with timely and relevant information from both theaters because of their access and understanding of the operational situation as CENTCOM representatives and were authorized to speak on behalf of the DoD.[145] In the past, this had been a major challenge in both Dubai and

Doha since the U.S. State Department was extremely leery of speaking on behalf of the DoD because they were not fully informed or aware of ongoing operations in either Afghanistan or Iraq. Given the fluidity of the news environment and the banning of *Al Jazeera* from Iraq, this team provided a short-term and solvent solution to assist the coalition in Iraq and *Al Jazeera* in Doha. This effort by the U.S. military, which yielded tangible results for *Al Jazeera*, coupled with a change in leadership of the Secretary of Defense, signaled a significant shift and helped foster improved relations with *Al Jazeera* at that period of time.

With the arrival of Robert Gates to the position of Secretary of Defense in December 2006, came a much greater appreciation for the role *Al Jazeera* played in communicating to the Middle East and the broader Muslim community. Gates' background and experience as the director for the CIA, coupled with his understanding of the broader challenges within the Middle East, namely Iran and Iraq, made him well aware of the impact and importance of *Al Jazeera* and other Arab press outlets in relation to public opinion in the region. Although not singling out any particular press entity, Gates espoused much greater outreach and engagement with the press corps than his predecessor. In a speech to the graduating class of the U.S. Naval Academy in May 2007, he affirmed this philosophy and reminded the midshipmen that "the press is not the enemy and to treat it as such is self-defeating."[146] Gates arrival also coincided with the newly launched *Al Jazeera-English* channel and its opening of a Washington, DC bureau. With the new bureau, *Al Jazeera-English* would also have access to the many Pentagon press briefings and to the various senior leaders within its halls. Gates would later participate in several interviews on *Al Jazeera-English* addressing a wide range of topics including: withdrawal from Iraq, strategy for peace in Afghanistan, operations against Al Qaeda in Iraq and Afghanistan and Iran's nuclear threat among several other topics.[147, 148]

Gates senior staff also supported a much greater outreach with the press in support of operations in Iraq. Augmenting the communications directorate in the Multi-National Force- Iraq headquarters with senior civilian public affairs specialists from the Pentagon, this decision greatly enhanced the coalition's ability to communicate with not just traditional news outlets, but also a much greater range of new media and blog writers, both remarkably new phenomena at that time in history. The "surge" in communication specialists in January and February of 2007 would precede the actual "surge" of troops that would arrive later that spring under the leadership of General David Petraeus. One of the most underreported aspects of the Iraq War was the impact these specialists had in communicating to both the domestic and international audiences.

As equally underappreciated was the coalition's deliberate effort to reach out to the Arabic press, specifically *Al Jazeera*. At that time in history, *Al Jazeera's* news bureau in Baghdad was closed at the direction of the Iraqi Government for allegedly fomenting discord among the Iraqi people and heightening the insurgency due to its news coverage. However, *Al Jazeera* was still being broadcast to the Iraqi people and far exceeded other networks in popularity among Iraqis. Given the country-wide ban on *Al Jazeera* in Iraq, the leadership of the communication directorate under then Major General William B. Caldwell, IV, was frustrated by the inability to interact with *Al*

Jazeera within Iraq and the strong tendency of the network to misreport information since they had such limited access. With Petraeus' approval Caldwell and a small team of communication specialists arranged to travel to Doha and the *Al Jazeera* headquarters in February 2007. The purpose behind the trip was two-fold; to conduct television interviews and to engage in a dialogue with the *Al Jazeera* senior leadership concerning some of the misreporting of information from the network. To the surprise of the team, they were warmly welcomed by the network's highest levels of leadership and engaged in two-plus hours of discussions on some of the major issues both sides were encountering. The meetings were made possible in large part due to the active outreach efforts of then, U.S. Army Captain Eric Clarke, who was part of the Dubai-based CENTCOM media outreach team. As Clarke mediated the dialogue, it was apparent the chief concern of the network was the Iraqi ban that was still in effect for its reporters. Caldwell listened attentively and offered to bring the network's request back to General Petraeus for his awareness and assistance. The coalition spokesman also participated in multiple interviews on both the Arabic and the newly launched English news channels. Although each interview challenged the coalition's assertions and data, each of the presenters also gave Caldwell ample opportunity to clarify or reinforce his points. Interestingly, the *Al Jazeera* leaders asked Caldwell to return the following month. Following the day's worth of engagements, Caldwell's team returned to Baghdad and discovered the appearances on both *Al Jazeera* channels were highly successful in communicating what needed to be shared with the world and even more successful in informing the Iraqi population. Additionally, through the private recommendations of Caldwell, General Petraeus was able to convince the Iraqi Government to reconsider its decision to ban *Al Jazeera* from reporting within Iraq. Within a month after the trip, the *Al Jazeera* chief correspondent in Baghdad was permitted to reenter the country and was allowed to begin reporting from within Iraq.

Given this outreach effort, the coalition also agreed to provide weekly interviews from Iraq using both satellite broadcasting capabilities in the U.S. Embassy and taped interviews with the *Al Jazeera* team in Baghdad. These interview opportunities proved to be an extremely critical component of the communication strategy as the "U.S. Surge" began to flow, as "Operation Fardh al Qanoon" was launched, and as the "Anbar Awakening" grew in prominence and effectiveness. The success of that first trip to Doha, led Caldwell back on three more occasions over the next four months, the last of which was in May 2007. The success of this new and constructive relationship with *Al Jazeera* was wholeheartedly embraced and championed by the U.S. DoD as a model for outreach.[149]

Meanwhile, the arrival of Admiral Michael "Mike" Mullen as the 17th Chairman of the Joint Chiefs of Staff in October 2007 also dramatically improved the Pentagon's willingness to do more outreach with *Al Jazeera*. The son of a Hollywood press agent[150] and a career naval officer, coupled with his recent duties as Commander, Allied Joint Force Command Naples, was highly aware of the strategic influence and importance of reaching out to both the domestic and international press corps, in order to better inform the world of the U.S. military's operations. Additionally, Mullen's public affairs officer, then-U.S. Navy Captain John Kirby, was also considered one the U.S. military's most respected and creative public affairs officers. His willingness to increase the Chairman's media profile through the use of social media like *You Tube* and *Twitter*[151] as well as a taking a more proactive approach to reaching out to more international news outlets like *Al Jazeera,* transformed the media presence of the new chairman and helped assuage many of the concerns between the Pentagon and *Al Jazeera.* Mullen, much like Secretary Gates was more than willing to interview with *Al Jazeera* and appeared in multiple programs throughout his tenure as Chairman.[152],[153] To their credit, these senior leaders' appearances on the various *Al Jazeera* programs were perceived as extremely positive by the *Al Jazeera* staff in spite of some of the most difficult topics and policy issues addressed by the presenters.[154]

Even with the evolving relationship under Gates' and Mullen's leadership and fresh outreach efforts with the *Al Jazeera* senior leadership in Doha, there were still significant challenges and barriers in the relationship, the largest of which was the U.S military's continued detention of Sami al-Hajj, one of *Al Jazeera's* international correspondents, who was stopped at the Afghanistan border by Pakistani authorities in December 2001 and was eventually turned over to U.S. forces and transported to the U.S. Detention Facility at Guantanamo Bay, Cuba. Al Hajj's detention continued to hamper the relationship as his *Al Jazeera* colleagues claimed his detention was "American harassment of an Arabic TV network whose coverage has long angered U.S. officials."[155] Although Al Hajj would be released without charge in May 2008, his detention continues to be one of many unresolved issues between the two institutions to this day. The other major concern from *Al Jazeera's* perspective at that time in history was the limited access the network had to DoD senior officials and spokespersons along with the DoD's lack of responsiveness to the network's many requests for public comments or interviews both at the Pentagon and on the battlefield. Recounting the prevailing attitude and posture of the Pentagon towards *Al Jazeera* at that time in history, Josh Rushing summed up his frustration: "Administration-appointed civilians at the Pentagon commonly forbid the military to speak to *Al Jazeera*, but the policymakers won't go on-air to defend their policies, either-thus leaving the network with the think-tank extremists from the right and the blogosphere idealists from the left. The resulting stories make Americans look like fools or cynics." [156]

In contrast to Rushing's assertions about the challenges within the walls of the Pentagon, there was growing support for *Al Jazeera* among the uniformed leaders of the military who were commanding forces in Iraq and Afghanistan and from those leaders charged with training and educating the next generation of leaders. Among them, Lieutenant General William Caldwell, who had the most personal experience with *Al Jazeera* while assigned as the chief military spokesman in Iraq. Based on his personal experiences and observations from his time in Iraq, Caldwell would become one of *Al Jazeera's* biggest advocates throughout the DoD as he pressed for greater outreach by our military's senior leadership with *Al Jazeera* and even spearheaded an effort to include *Al Jazeera-English* in the cable television channels offered throughout the U.S. Army's Command and General Staff College at Fort Leavenworth, Kansas shortly after he assumed command there.[157] Caldwell also appeared regularly on *Al Jazeera's* programming over the next several years culminating with an extensive interview on *Al Jazeera-English* in conjunction with his departure from command in Afghanistan in November 2011.[158] Caldwell was not alone in his support for the growing network.

Now retired General Stanley McChrystal, chose to conduct an interview with *Al Jazeera-English* on the same day of his congressional testimony regarding progress in Afghanistan in December 2009. McChrystal's interview with Riz Khan in the Washington, DC studio of *Al Jazeera* was so effective that it prompted the U.S. State Department to request a similar interview for Secretary of State Hilary Clinton.[159] Of note, prior to the interview, Khan actually singled out Lieutenant General Caldwell for his previous visit to the studio and also for Caldwell's desire to have new recruits watch *Al Jazeera* to gain a better international perspective.[160]

Another strong advocate for *Al Jazeera* was Brigadier General Mark Kimmit, also a former spokesman for the U.S. military forces in Iraq and a leader who was at the heart of criticism directed against *Al Jazeera* for what he alleged was inaccurate, biased and inflammatory reporting in April 2004.[161] Just two years after his assertions about the network's biased reporting in Iraq, Kimmit would be the first American general officer to appear live in the *Al Jazeera* studios in Doha, where he addressed a wide range of topics regarding the Middle East in a very contentious interview.[162] To Kimmit's credit, he seemed to be one of only a handful of military officers who recognized the importance of reaching out to *Al Jazeera* at a time when many others were avoiding any contact with the network. Kimmit's willingness to participate in interviews and discussions with the network would also serve him well out of uniform as he transitioned into his next posting as the U.S. Assistant Secretary of State for Political-Military Affairs. Since that first interview, Kimmit has been a frequent guest on *Al Jazeera's* programming addressing topics ranging from withdrawal of forces in Iraq to the strategic impacts for the United States in the wake of the killing of Osama bin Laden. Kimmit's active participation and transformation from "*Al Jazeera* critic" to a frequent "*Al Jazeera* guest commentator" suggests there may be greater recognition among other senior military leaders of *Al Jazeera* as a valuable global news source well as highlight the need for greater participation from the DoD's current senior leaders to address some of the same questions Kimmit is frequently asked.

In addition to these three senior leaders advocating for greater engagement with *Al Jazeera* by the DoD, there also seemed to be a growing group of other military leaders forward deployed in Afghanistan, who saw the network with a new perspective and recognized the need for a more active approach.[163] When asked why he chose to watch *Al Jazeera* in lieu of *CNN* or other American cable news channels, one American senior military officer stated "because it is real news that is relevant to our mission and Afghanistan, not just America. I would rather know what is going on in the world rather than what someone in Hollywood is doing."[164] This officer's opinion seemed to also be indicative of the majority of other senior and junior leaders serving in Afghanistan as evidenced by their preference for watching *Al Jazeera* in their offices and monitoring of the *Al Jazeera* websites for news updates to the Commanding General.

Today, although there have been laudatory comments and a much greater willingness to engage in interviews and conversation with *Al Jazeera* by senior American officials in the White House, Congress, and the State Department, this same attitude has not been matched by the senior leaders within the DoD since Gates and Mullen's departure in 2011. Unfortunately, there does appear to be a clear drop in participation on *Al Jazeera's* programming by any of the current Pentagon leadership.

By reviewing *Al Jazeera's* database of interviews with senior defense leaders (Secretary of Defense, Chairman of the Joint Chiefs of Staff, and Service Chiefs) there is a clear lack of presence on *Al Jazeera* when compared to their participation in interviews with other major news networks namely *CNN* and *BBC.*[165] Moreover, recent discussions and correspondence with several members of the *Al Jazeera-English* news bureau in Washington, D.C. confirmed the same observations. Although there have been noticeable improvements in recognition of *Al Jazeera* as a quality news provider throughout the Pentagon, there has been a noticeable absence from any of its programming by current and former DoD senior leadership in the last two years.[166] While Admiral Jonathan Greenert, Chief of Naval Operations (CNO) appeared in March 2012, none of the other current senior leadership in the Pentagon has appeared in *Al Jazeera* taped or live interviews during their current posting. Prior to Greenert's appearance, Admiral Mullen, former Chairman of the Joint Chiefs of Staff appeared in January 2011, and Robert Gates, former Secretary of Defense appeared in both June 2010 and September 2009.[167] Since that time, only Greenert has represented the top leadership of the Pentagon on any of *Al Jazeera's* programs. However positive the efforts of these senior leaders may have been, the question being asked is "where are the other senior DoD leaders?" and "why have they not taken a more proactive approach in dialoguing with, appearing on *Al Jazeera's* programs, and encouraging their subordinate leaders to do the same." [168] In spite of its growing credibility and popularity, it is unknown why there still exists a natural aversion by civilian and military leaders within DoD to engage with *Al Jazeera* in either on-camera interviews or in private meetings.

So why the current resistance? Is it institutional, doctrinal, or political?

Although some have surmised the reason for the lack of engagement by the current leadership of the DoD is because of the residual feelings of animosity and resentment for *Al Jazeera* that may still be prevalent within the Pentagon.[169] It is unclear if the negative public statements about *Al Jazeera* by Donald Rumsfeld and his open disregard of the network during his term as Secretary of Defense have had a lasting effect on the Pentagon. Given many of the civilian and military public affairs specialists charged with the DoD's media relations tend to remain or return to the Pentagon, it is feasible that many were present during Rumsfeld's tenure and they may still harbor reservations of the network. Therefore, their influence and willingness to support interviews with the network may still be tainted by the experiences and practices of the "Rumsfeld Era". However, this theory does not explain the improved relations that occurred immediately after Rumsfeld's resignation and the subsequent improved relations with *Al Jazeera* under Secretary Gates and Admiral Mullen's leadership of the Pentagon. Additionally, many of the senior uniformed public affairs officers now advising the senior leadership of the DoD have had operational experience within the last 10 years of their careers in either Afghanistan or Iraq and this experience would probably warrant greater consideration of engagement with *Al Jazeera* as opposed to disregarding the network.

Another reason may lie in the DoD's own institutional policies, doctrine and publications, which have created a perception that engagement with *Al Jazeera* and other international news organizations is the responsibility of the U.S. State Department and not the DoD's. Traditionally, within the United States engagement with international news outlets had in fact been the primary responsibility of the U.S. State Department, while the DoD focused principally on the domestic press. However, current joint doctrine clearly articulates the importance of engagement with international media and audiences. It states: "The U.S. military has an obligation to communicate with the American public, and it is in the national interest to communicate with the international public."[170] Moreover, it also suggests that engagement with international press may be more critical than even the domestic press in some circumstances and at some points in time: "International interest in military operations may be just as high, and sometimes higher, than US media interest, especially in military operations conducted overseas."[171] Since the DoD's own doctrine recognizes the importance of outreach to international press like *Al Jazeera*, the rationale that it is the U.S. State Department's responsibility to interact with *Al Jazeera* and not the DoD's is not supported by either joint doctrine or the individual service publications. In fact, each calls for greater interaction with foreign press. Dr. Hy Rothstein of the Naval Postgraduate School also concurs with joint doctrine and refutes the idea that the State Department holds carte blanche on engagement with international press outlets like *Al Jazeera*. He asserts: "Given the State Department's limited manning, resources, and experience with military operations, they are ill-equipped and ill-prepared to communicate with the press on behalf of the DoD."[172]

Another explanation for the lack of engagement with *Al Jazeera* may also be a product of timing and recent U.S domestic issues, namely the U.S Presidential Election and subsequent focus on budgetary challenges of the Sequestration. Traditionally, it has become common place within the DoD during presidential election years to limit media exposure of its top officials to minimize perceptions of partisanship or tacit support for either the incumbent or the challenger. Given the hotly contested and highly volatile U.S election of 2012, it is a reasonable assumption the Pentagon's top leaders sought to avoid frequent appearances on domestic news programs, especially during the months leading up to the election in November 2012. Although this may account for a drop in domestic news appearances, it does not explain the lack of participation with *Al Jazeera* and other international news programs since their focus would almost certainly be geared towards foreign policy or military strategy. In recent months, it also appears the DoD senior leadership have had a singularly-focused strategy of articulating the impacts of the government sequestration, a decision which could have potentially devastating effects on the U.S. military for years to come. This singular focus equates to limited media appearances on programs that desire to discuss topics of broader strategic or international impact. Instead, there have been more appearances by these senior leaders on domestic programming in order to highlight the challenges associated with defense budget cuts. With good reason this communication strategy would be logical given the long-term negative consequences they believe the sequestration would have on the DoD writ large. However, this rationale would only account for the period of time from January to present when the senior leadership has in fact been making frequent appearances on many news programs, none of which were *Al Jazeera* programs. Even if this was true, it does not account for the lack of participation with *Al Jazeera* prior to this period.

Some also suggested it may be because of lack of understanding of, experience with or recognition of *Al Jazeera* as a valuable news provider.[173] There are many senior leaders and public affairs professionals who openly claim they have watched *Al Jazeera's* programming and prefer it over the other global news networks, yet very few of these same individuals have ever interacted or interviewed with *Al Jazeera*.[174] Although there is growing recognition within the DoD, there is still a significant lack of understanding and an even greater lack of education for its senior leaders and public affairs professionals of *Al Jazeera.* In the absence of understanding or education, there is minimal desire to reach out and do more. This perhaps is the strongest explanation for the current leadership's posture with *Al Jazeera*, although that may significantly change with the arrival of the new Secretary of Defense, Chuck Hagel, considered to be a supportive voice for the network and an individual who has previously appeared on *Al Jazeera* programming.[175]

IV. Implications for the DoD: Time for change and the rationale behind greater engagement with *Al Jazeera*

Regardless of the reasons for the lack of engagement that have governed the past, given the changing nature of the U.S. defense strategy from an operational focus in Afghanistan and Iraq, to globally integrated operations, along with a change in Pentagon senior leadership, perhaps a shift in communication strategy is also necessitated. Recognizing the importance of information, the Capstone Concept for Joint Operations (CCJO) highlights the operational challenges it presents: "The ubiquity of personal communications devices with cameras and full motion video also allows much of the world to observe unfolding events in real time, rendering future operations increasingly sensitive to popular perceptions. As we have learned in Iraq and Afghanistan, military actions will receive intense media scrutiny, a dynamic that potentially invests otherwise inconsequential actions with strategic importance."[176] Whereas in the past, DoD public affairs could principally focus their media relations efforts on domestic audiences and issues, today's global realities and pervasive information environment require renewed emphasis on engagement with global news networks that have the capacity and credibility to inform and educate international audiences of DoD's strategy, policies, and operations. For several reasons, *Al Jazeera* represents a viable option for the DoD as it seeks to broaden its outreach efforts and as it seeks to communicate and achieve the objectives of this new strategy.

***Al Jazeera's* Expanding Reach and Global Presence**

In an era where the U.S. Defense Strategy calls for greater global presence by strengthening "its presence in the Asia Pacific region and continued vigilance in the Middle East,"[177] increased engagement with *Al Jazeera* offers a viable means to help achieve these objectives. In contrast to its major competitors, *Al Jazeera* has sought to achieve a stronger global presence. Since its modest beginnings in a building that housed less than 150 employees and broadcasting to an audience of less than a million viewers, *Al Jazeera* today operates more than 70 news bureaus across the world, the majority of which are located in Africa, Asia and both Central and Latin America. By comparison, CNN has closed many of its international bureaus and today it only maintains 45 editorial operations, 14 of which are located in the U.S.[178] *Al Jazeera* today employs more than 3,000 staff members across the globe, including more than

400 journalists from more than 60 different countries. *Al Jazeera-English,* the largest of the many *Al Jazeera* channels, employs "more than 1,200 highly experienced staff from more than 50 nationalities, making *Al Jazeera-English's* newsroom among the most diverse in the world." [179] Operating from its Doha headquarters and two different news centers 24 hours a day/seven days a week, *Al Jazeera* now broadcasts into more than 130 different countries (over 2/3 of the world's countries) in multiple languages including: Arabic, English, Bosnian, and Serbo-Croatian with plans to expand to a Turkish channel later this year.[180] Renowned author, professor, and Director of the Center on Public Diplomacy at the University of Southern California, Philip Seib sees *Al Jazeera*'s growth and impact as much more than just a Middle Eastern phenomenon: "The Qatar based station has played a historic role in transforming media not only in the Middle East but also globally, proving that the hegemony of the predominantly Western media establishment can be successfully challenged. Beyond *Al Jazeera*'s own success in this regard, the channel serves as a model within the Arab world and beyond, an example of news organizations with regional and global reach that are certain to proliferate during the next decade."[181]

Al Jazeera also has significantly more coverage of global issues as opposed to recent trends within U.S.-based media to narrow its international news coverage. According to the Pew Research Center's 2012 Annual State of the News Media Report, CNN devoted only about 34% of its coverage to international events and matters that concerned U.S. involvement abroad. "The percentage was considerably less, 20%, on Fox and even smaller, 14%, on MSNBC."[182] Additionally, *Al Jazeera* tends to focus more of its news coverage on issues affecting those areas of the world that are often overlooked by the majority of news networks, yet have proven to a challenge for the United States and its foreign policy. One of *Al Jazeera's* founding editorial philosophies was to cover news stories from those areas of the world that are typically underreported namely Africa, Asia, Latin America and the Middle East or the "Global South". Seeing this as an opportunity to reverse the normal flow and filtering of information from the Global North (namely the U.S. and Europe) to the Global South, *Al Jazeera* has markedly outdistanced its competitors in this effort. Tine Ustad Figenschou, a Postdoctoral Fellow at the University of Oslo found that "*Al Jazeera- English* covered the South with in-depth news formats (offering reflection, discussion, and background information) more frequently than it did the North."[183] Her findings, coupled with the newly directed U.S. strategic guidance to focus on the "challenges and opportunities" present in the Asia Pacific and "political and economic reform" in the Middle East and North Africa,[184] suggest *Al Jazeera* can play a significant role in understanding and communicating with the citizens of those nations that are considered of strategic interest to the United States. Although these areas traditionally also have the highest potential for conflict and crisis, U.S. domestic news coverage is usually minimal or non-existent until conflict escalates or crises begin to unfold. The usual response from U.S. networks is to send a small team of journalists into the area and begin reporting on the crisis with little or no knowledge of the environment, the diversity of the culture or the actual root causes of the crisis. Given even greater fiscal challenges for U.S. news outlets, this type of "parachute journalism" has actually increased within the last five years. By contrast, *Al Jazeera*-English, for example, prides itself on citizen journalism and hiring more local correspondents to highlight the challenges within the "Global South" and other underreported regions of the globe.

Al Jazeera's expanding global presence is also marked by greater and more rapid cross sharing of information between its various news channels as evidenced by its coverage of the Arab Spring. Taking live footage from both citizen journalists and its own correspondents in Tunisia, Libya, Yemen, and Egypt, *Al Jazeera* was able to rebroadcast it in multiple languages on multiple channels across the world before its nearest competitors causing many U.S. based news providers to just rebroadcast *Al Jazeera*'s footage. Its remarkable access at multiple key sites of the Arab Spring gave it a marked competitive advantage over its nearest business rival and dramatically improved its credibility across the globe, especially within the U.S Government. This access continues to expand as it seeks to further broaden its global presence both in establishment of news bureaus as well as expansion of its citizen journalist reporting within countries that are emerging as potential areas of conflict.

Given its increasing global footprint, its focus on areas considered of greater strategic interest, and the sizeable presence of its worldwide news bureaus, *Al Jazeera* possesses unmatched access and ability to communicate timely news content of vital importance to the DoD and its allies, especially in light of evolving U.S. Defense Strategy and fiscal constraints.

***Al Jazeera*'s Greater Respect Among Key Audiences and Marginalized Groups**

Al Jazeera's greatest strength may be its ability to provide global viewers with a different perspective than most of the western-based television news networks (i.e.

CNN, *BBC*, *Sky News*) can provide and a perspective that is more closely aligned with its primary viewership. Contrary to many who believe *Al Jazeera* is limited to providing an Arab perspective for Arab viewers, its senior leadership asserts it has broadened its perspectives and appeals to a much wider audience. James Wright, executive producer of one of *Al Jazeera*-English's newest and most popular programs, "The Stream," offered his thoughts on the topic. He offered: "I have never had the sense that we are providing an "Arab perspective' nor is there one single Arab perspective. We look to provide all sides to a story – there are many opinions within the Arab community and we look to provide those along with the views of other communities. For its English channel, *Al Jazeera* provides a much broader global perspective."[185]

As a result, *Al Jazeera* has attracted one of the most loyal audiences and exerts unmatched influence over its viewers' global perspective when compared to other news organizations. This is primarily due to its strict adherence to its foundational principles as well as its unique appeal to Muslim viewers worldwide. Chief among these principles is the concept of reporting both sides of every story. In its adoption of the motto "the opinion and the other opinion" and creating programs that were "intended to stimulate debate and controversy", *Al Jazeera's* leadership challenged the status quo of Middle Eastern media and the absolute power of authoritarian governments.[186] To achieve this, the network continues to maintain objectivity and balance by providing a variety of programming marked by diverse viewpoints and opinions. Unlike other media outlets within the Middle East, *Al Jazeera* sought to open dialogue on some of the most controversial topics in the Arab world such as: government corruption, sex, and many other previously considered prohibited topics. Offering Israeli officials full live and taped interviews, *Al Jazeera* became both loved and hated for its decision to break from a long held taboo in Arab media.[187] By continuing to offer programming featuring "the opinion and the other opinion" coupled with its expansion to an English news channel, *Al Jazeera* has even attracted a significant amount of loyal followers well beyond the Middle East.

Another principle that has dramatically bolstered *Al Jazeera*'s audience loyalty is its proclamation to serve as "the voice of the voiceless". By highlighting many of the ills of the global society and the lives of those who suffer as a result, especially those who perceive themselves as disenfranchised, *Al Jazeera* has dramatically improved its appeal to viewers. By avoiding the commentary and public statements from those who are perceived as being in power, *Al Jazeera* seeks to bring out the human interest perspective of every story including civilian casualties from war, starving families in refugee camps, and widowed spouses of police officers. By offering the poorest peasant the same platform as the richest ruler, *Al Jazeera's* desire to give a voice to the voiceless has increased its audience, improved its credibility and enhanced its global opportunities especially in the wake of its coverage of the Arab Spring.

Along with significant audience loyalty and appeal, *Al Jazeera* is widely popular and wields tremendous influence within the worldwide Muslim community, a community that the DoD and U.S. Government writ large have struggled to communicate with. In fact, recent findings by the Pew Research Center suggest, Muslim countries opinion of U.S. policies have actually decreased by 19 percentage points from a similar study in 2009.[188] By contrast, *Al Jazeera* enjoys relative popularity and trust within these same countries. Because *Al Jazeera*'s audience demographics vary widely depending on the channel being watched, studies of *Al Jazeera*'s audience are extremely limited and complex. However, a 2004 study by Philip Auter and associates suggested the average viewer of *Al Jazeera* programming is typically a relatively young, well-educated, financially stable married Muslim male. Of note, the 5,000 plus respondents representing 137 different countries "watched *Al Jazeera* for hours on end - or at least keep the network on in the background while doing other things - keeping it on for nearly half their waking hours." [189] In another study conducted on the perceptions of *Al Jazeera-Arabic's* viewers, researchers found *Al Jazeera* viewers typically were more critical of U.S. foreign policy. However, that same study showed the majority of viewers who watched *Al Jazeera* tended to be better informed and open to dialogue with the West.[190]

Although there are multiple Arabic channels and global news networks prevalent throughout the Middle East and beyond, *Al Jazeera* continues to be the preferred network viewed by the majority of Muslims across the world. According to author and Middle Eastern affairs expert, Dr. Glenn Robinson, "the data I have seen shows that not only is *Al Jazeera* by far the most watched source of regional and international news among all Arabs (at about 50%), *Al Jazeera* is also the most trusted source of news in the Arab and Muslim worlds."[191]It has achieved this in large part due to its ability to serve as a unifier of Arab voices and portray itself as the voice for Arabs and Muslims worldwide. In the eyes of authors El-Nawawy and Iskandar: "No Arab satellite TV network other than *Al Jazeera* has ever attempted to present Arab views, opinions, and beliefs to the West with such vigor and legitimacy."[192]

Given these findings, it is clear *Al Jazeera* appeals to audiences that the DoD should also be striving to communicate with. These audiences, contrary to many assertions by pundits and various spokespersons with hidden agendas are not ignorant or uninformed. Although critical of U.S. policy, they are typically better informed of the broader issues affecting those policies. Therefore, it would be more appropriate for the DoD to communicate its strategies and policies through *Al Jazeera* rather than with other networks. *Al Jazeera's* ability to serve as a powerful and influential communicator to audiences that are typically hostile or non-supportive to U.S. foreign policy and military operations necessitates greater engagement by our DoD leadership and by those who serve with them.

***Al Jazeera*'s Increasing Role as an Agenda Setter and Global Influencer**

Since its inception, *Al Jazeera* has seen itself as an important instrument for affecting change and setting the news agenda. In a region beset with regimented and highly censored journalism, *Al Jazeera* sought to change the way Arab journalism was performed in the Middle East and in so doing it would also change the politics of the region as well. Leveraging the power of public opinion, it also sought to present the Arab perspective to the world; a world that had previously only viewed the Middle East through a Western perspective such as *CNN* or *BBC. Al Jazeera* has dramatically changed that perspective and is continuing to affect public opinion and reach a broader audience as it expands its own global footprint.

Chief among its many advantages it currently enjoys over its competitors is its ability to serve as an "agenda setter" in the Middle East. Advocating itself as a "voice for the voiceless", it continues to tackle the most controversial of issues in some of the most restrictive environments. Whereas in the past, governments and regimes could limit voices that did not serve their agendas, today's unfettered access to the internet and satellite television has allowed *Al Jazeera* and other news outlets to set many domestic and international agendas regardless of the government's support or not. Adel Iskandar, author and adjunct instructor at Georgetown University on Arab media and Middle Eastern affairs feels: "In many ways they [*Al Jazeera*] set the agenda in the Arab world."[193] Although there is no question of *Al Jazeera's* unmatched influence in affecting the agenda within the Middle East and the broader Muslim community, with the expansion of *Al Jazeera-English* and the establishment of broadcasting centers in Doha, Kuala Lumpur, London and Washington DC along with countless bureaus worldwide, the network hopes to set the global news agenda by "bridging cultures and providing a unique grassroots perspective from under-reported regions around the world to a potential global audience of over one billion English speakers." [194] With its arrival to America and launch of *Al Jazeera-America*, it also hopes to build upon its past successes and have a noticeable effect on the U.S. domestic agenda as well. Given it's unmatched ability to set the agenda in the Middle East, its growing capacity in setting the global agenda and its expanding American market, *Al Jazeera* represents the most significant voice of influence within global media outlets.

Al Jazeera has also proven itself to be a powerful influence for political mobilization, a phenomenon the DoD should be well aware of as it views the ongoing crisis in Syria and Mali and determines an appropriate strategy for engagement. *Al Jazeera-English's* coverage of the Arab Spring provided viewers with unprecedented access to both the protestor and reporter's perspectives from the various sites of the ongoing revolutions. In writing about the Arab Spring and *Al Jazeera's* role, Will Youmans suggested: "*Al Jazeera-English* practiced a type of networked journalism that let protestors and local reporters share their views and information with the rest of the world. This offset somewhat governments' strictures on reporters and efforts to control news flow."[195] Leveraging the latest technologies and platforms for social media, *Al Jazeera* quickly became the go-to channel for viewers, mobile-phone owners, and internet users around the world. Much like CNN in the Gulf War of 1991, *Al Jazeera* and its affiliates were able to capture a significant portion of global viewership in the midst of unfolding events in the Middle East, especially *Al Jazeera-English*, who some believed helped break through many of the ruling governments best propaganda attempts. Coining the phrase "the *Al Jazeera* Effect" years prior to the actual Arab Spring, Philip Seib viewed the network as one several forms of new media that would have significant global and regional influence in the political landscape. He stated: "the Arab satellite channel itself is just the most visible player in a huge universe of new communications and information providers that are changing the relationship between those who govern and those who are governed. It is also assisting those with previously unachievable political agendas. The advent of television a half-century ago pales in comparison with new media's effects on global political life today."[196] His comments proved to be visionary as *Al Jazeera* and *Al Jazeera-English* transformed the Arab Spring into an international reform movement bringing very different groups of people from around the world together in unity in support of the uprisings. Youmans also believed: "It also arguably privileged online activists by giving them coverage and rebroadcasting their content, which empowered them to define and frame the uprisings in their terms."[197] Understanding *Al Jazeera's* effect on political mobilization should be of paramount importance as the DoD seeks to better understand its own future roles and missions across the globe, whether it be geographical or in the cyber domain.

Additionally, *Al Jazeera* has enjoyed a marked increase in its worldwide acceptance and credibility as a professional news provider as evidenced by the dramatic increase in the awards and honors it has received from various global news organizations since its inception. Of note, in 2012 alone, *Al Jazeera-English* received as many awards (20) as it had from 2006-2010 primarily for its reporting of the Arab Spring.[198] Notable among all of its awards was the 2011Columbia University Journalism Award, which is given annually to recognize an individual or organization for "singular journalism in the public interest."[199] Marking only the second time the award was given to an organization, the School of Journalism's dean, Nicholas Lemann saluted *Al Jazeera-English* for "its determination to get to the heart of a complicated story unfolding in countries where news has historically been difficult to cover."[200] Moreover, many of its recent awards are from organizations that are based in the United States or the United Kingdom, suggesting further acceptance of *Al Jazeera* in markets that had traditionally been hindered by political and public opposition to its coverage. *Al Jazeera* is also exceeding its nearest competitors in global influence in brand name alone. In a 2006 survey by BrandChannel.com, it ranked *Al Jazeera* higher than either of its major competitors for its global impact. The findings of this study according to Josh Rushing make *Al Jazeera* "arguably the most influential news brand across the world."[201] It is a reasonable assumption *Al Jazeera's* brand influence and impact has also considerably increased given this study was conducted prior to the start up of *Al Jazeera-English* in late 2006.

Given *Al Jazeera's* ever-expanding global presence and access, its strong relationship and unmatched appeal to key audiences and marginalized communities, and its increasing role as an agenda setter and global influencer perhaps now is the time for DoD's senior leadership to take a more proactive and positive approach with *Al Jazeera* and its affiliated news channels. Based on the countless reasons in support of greater engagement between the two institutions, the question must not be "should we do more?", but "how can we do more?"

V. Moving From a Culture of Estrangement to a Culture of Engagement: Recommendations for the Department of Defense

In consideration of *Al Jazeera's* growing audience and influence, broad appeal to diverse audiences worldwide, coupled with the changing nature of the U.S. Military Defense Strategy and its senior leadership, the findings suggest the need for DoD's senior leadership to foster a proactive culture of engagement with *Al Jazeera* and its affiliated news channels. In order to remove any institutional resistance to future engagement with the network and its affiliated channels, it is recommended the DoD adopt a strategy focused on increased education, graduated exposure and active participation. The key to any strategy will be the willingness of the senior leadership to embrace it, enforce it and empower others to execute it.

Increased Education: The Key to Rebuilding the Relationship

In the spirit of Abraham Lincoln's famous quote, "I don't like that man. I must get to know him better,"[202] the most important step the DoD and its senior leaders can take to foster a culture of engagement with *Al Jazeera* is to learn more about an organization that most do not fully understand nor appreciate. The simplest way to accomplish this is through face to face meetings with the senior leadership of *Al Jazeera* both in Doha and in the *Al Jazeera* Bureau in Washington, D.C. This seemingly easy step will probably be the most difficult given scheduling and travel challenges of the senior leadership of the DoD. However, it will undoubtedly be the most rewarding as it demonstrates a willingness to listen and the resolve to move toward a more amenable relationship as demonstrated by former Secretary of State Hillary Clinton in 2010, when she arranged her itinerary to build time for meeting with senior leadership at the *Al Jazeera* headquarters in Doha.[203]

Similarly, DOD's senior leadership could also find an executive level meeting like this to be extremely beneficial to understanding some of the major challenges the network has faced in the relationship and most importantly, dialogue about ways to address the challenges of the past. This simple step by the DoD senior leadership to reach out to *Al Jazeera* and meet with its top leaders at their headquarters would send a strong message of support and demonstrate a sincere willingness to work more cooperatively in the future not only to the *Al Jazeera* team, but also to the rest of the DoD and its subordinate leaders, both civilian and military leaders alike. Although the DoD international media relations team should spearhead the coordination of this effort, the DoD executive staff must be active participants as well to ensure adequate time and resources are directed to support the meeting. If traveling to its headquarters in Doha is too problematic or doesn't align with senior DoD leadership overseas travel itineraries, a secondary option would be for a similar meeting to occur at the *Al Jazeera* news bureau in Washington, DC. Although the representative audience would not be as senior on the *Al Jazeera* side, the message would still signal a strong desire to work more cooperatively in the future. Whether in Doha or DC, all conversations between the senior leadership of both organizations should be informal and strictly "off the record", serving as trust builders between both organizations. This initial meeting with *Al Jazeera* could also serve to be an opportune time for the DoD senior leaders to see firsthand how the *Al Jazeera* news is made and how it is transmitted to the wide variety of *Al Jazeera* channels. Key to this initial meeting will be follow up and further exposure to the network for DoD's senior leadership.

Beyond education and introduction of the DoD senior leaders and the various service senior leaders throughout the Pentagon, the Joint Services should broaden the current educational experiences in media relations at various levels of Professional Military Education (PME) for its company and field grade officers and senior non-commissioned officers to include *Al Jazeera* into their curricula as well. There are numerous examples of how this could be successfully accomplished with minimal impact and maximal results namely: media panels, guest lectures, staff group/seminar visits or video teleconference (VTC) with *Al Jazeera* correspondents, staff or leaders. Since it has become common practice at almost every level of PME, to schedule a media panel or invite members of the press corps to deliver remarks to the students, faculty and staff, course schedulers could request *Al Jazeera* in lieu of requesting the same journalists as previous years or hosting only U.S.-based media panels. Inviting *Al Jazeera* to participate in a venue such as an international media panel at the U.S. Army War College would certainly spur intense debate and dialogue during the event, but it could also serve as superb opportunity to educate the next group of Army senior leaders about *Al Jazeera's* philosophies and methodologies. It could also go a long way in helping to assuage many of the stereotypes and individual biases both sides might have about each other.

The final aspect of the education process would be an introduction and information exchange with the DoD's public affairs professionals. As the DoD's principal staff for the execution of public affairs (PA), there are very few public affairs officers (PAOs) who have had regular exposure to the *Al Jazeera* staff or who have actively worked with any of its correspondents. For those who have, most see the need for greater engagement.[204] For the remainder of the PA professionals, the DoD could help foster increased understanding and improved relations by establishing routine outreach trips and meetings with PA senior leaders who are attending the Defense Information School (DINFOS) at Fort Meade, Maryland. Given the school's proximity to Washington, DC and routine scheduling of day trips to meet with Pentagon officials, perhaps replacing a portion of the Pentagon tour with a visit to *Al Jazeera's* DC bureau would yield greater understanding and awareness of the network by those charged with media relations and public communication. If not feasible, inviting *Al Jazeera* leaders or correspondents like Josh Rushing to meet with students at DINFOS would also help broaden the PA field's understanding and awareness of *Al Jazeera.* Further educational and career broadening experiences for mid-level PAOs could include consideration of *Al Jazeera* as a "Training with Industry" or TWI host. Given limited funding for these types of opportunities in the near future, current practices of sending officers to high cost of living areas such as New York City, Chicago and Palo Alto, California could be replaced by offering officers already assigned to the Pentagon, a six-nine month intern opportunity with *Al Jazeera-English* in the DC area. This effort would not require an officer and his/her family to move and could be followed by a utilization tour within the Pentagon and the international media relations team.

Regardless of the level of the outreach and education, any outreach by the DoD's senior leadership with *Al Jazeera* would be a marked step in the right direction for the DoD in its effort to establish a more proactive and positive relationship with *Al Jazeera;* a relationship that would greatly benefit both organizations.

<u>Graduated Exposure: The Key to Reinforcing the Relationship</u>

The key to reinforcing the new relationship with *Al Jazeera* will be for the DoD senior leadership and other leaders throughout the Joint Services to also be gradually exposed to more opportunities for dialogue and discussion with *Al Jazeera* and its various leaders.

Once the initial introductory meetings are completed, future senior leader engagements could be scheduled including office calls within the Pentagon with the respective service chiefs and their staffs. This would also afford an opportunity to showcase the DoD media relations team and further educate its talented group of civilian and military specialists. This not only affords *Al Jazeera* the opportunity to meet with the Pentagon's "Gatekeepers" of news information, but it also exposes *Al Jazeera* to the Pentagon team, many of whom have probably never personally met with any *Al Jazeera* employees. This second group of meetings should further expand as needed to follow on engagements as required, but consistency and graduated exposure will be essential. Unfortunately the network is somewhat jaded to the Pentagon's efforts to reestablish positive relations with it, given the DoD's lack of maintaining consistent contact as evidenced by the findings of one of its senior commanders. While visiting the *Al Jazeera-English* headquarters in 2011, Lieutenant General Caldwell was disappointed to learn that in spite of his and other senior leaders' efforts in late 2007 to open up routine channels of communication between the two organizations, there had been little to no follow up to the meetings he had conducted previously while assigned to the Multi-National Force in Iraq.[205] Caldwell and his staff found the leadership to be very open to greater engagement and interaction between the two organizations in spite of this clear lack of follow up to previous meetings. These leaders were also very interested in establishing regular operational and strategic updates with U.S. military leaders in Afghanistan, a desire that was shared with the International Security Assistance Force (ISAF) command upon the group's return to Afghanistan.[206] As of today, it is unclear if the command there has conducted any further follow up with *Al Jazeera*.

For both parties, the next logical step in reinforcing the relationship would be for the DoD senior leadership to participate in a more structured event such as an editorial board (gathering of the various news producers and regional news directors if available). The format is certainly open to preference, but typically these types of engagements are most beneficial to both sides if they are done "on background" to allow for in depth discussions of topics requiring significant context and explanation. These types of engagements are also very helpful for the news producers to gain a better perspective on the DoD's challenges, the policies governing the issues and what is being down to address the issue (i.e. suicide rates in the U.S. military, women in combat, sexual assault). This type of dialogue and venue also demonstrates a willingness to be open and transparent, while at the same affords the opportunity to hear the context and the details of the various issues without the constraints of time or the intimidation of a news camera. Follow on events like this should also be offered to the various service chiefs and the respective chief's of information or public affairs. As the services supposed subject matter experts on public affairs, the latter individuals would greatly benefit from building these types of engagements into their calendars on a quarterly or semi-annual basis.

At the operational level, given the effectiveness of the small Dubai-based media outreach team from 2006-2007, perhaps there should be further consideration by the USCENTCOM leadership of reestablishing something similar. Unlike what occurred shortly after General Petraeus took command of USCENTCOM, where the military members were replaced by U.S. Government contractors, who were not authorized to speak on the record on behalf of the DoD, the team should be manned by senior U.S. military members, who have the broad experience in and strategic understanding of the various DoD issues that might be of interest to *Al Jazeera* and its viewership. Given USCENTCOM, much like the other combatant commands, may be limited in its ability to man this type of operation, the DoD should consider earmarking public affairs professionals who would meet the above criteria. Given the criticality of language and culture throughout the Middle East, one additional consideration would be to consider providing these military leaders with Arabic language training to help them better communicate and work with not just the *Al Jazeera* leadership in Doha, but also the other Arab press outlets throughout the Gulf Region. This team's primary purpose would be to build and maintain relationships with these various media outlets through close proximity and sustained engagement.

At the senior education level, one potential event that would help build upon previous introduction to *Al Jazeera*, would be the *Al Jazeera* hosted visit by senior officers from the U.S. Army Senior Service Colleges (SSC). Given *Al Jazeera's* Washington, DC news bureau and its proximity to both the U.S. Army War College and the National Defense University, it would require minimal resources and travel time to organize such an event for those officers who are either senior communicators or are assuming command following their tenure at the respective SSCs. Exposing these officers to the *Al Jazeera* newsroom and its key correspondents and editors, would greatly enhance their understanding of not just *Al Jazeera*, but the nature of the global news networks in general. It would also help these officers to build individual relationships with key leaders of the *Al Jazeera* staff that may prove to be beneficial at a later time in their careers.

These are but a few examples of measures the DoD could implement to expand upon the relationship with *Al Jazeera* and to allow its senior leaders and key communicators the opportunity to have greater exposure with *Al Jazeera's* leadership and its programming.

Active Participation: The Key to Maintaining the Relationship

It has been said, "the proof is in the pudding." Given this statement, whether the relationship continues to remain positive between the two institutions will in large part be determined by the willingness of DoD's senior leadership to actively participate in interviews with *Al Jazeera* when they are requested or needed. Given the highly competitive and rapidly evolving nature of the news, it becomes paramount for DoD's senior leaders to make themselves available for on camera interviews with *Al Jazeera*, especially when news stories are breaking that may have significant strategic impact for the U.S. or the DoD. Unfortunately, the U.S. Government and the DoD's lack of response when it comes to *Al Jazeera's* requests for spokespeople can have negative strategic consequences or misrepresent the issue in question. Since *Al Jazeera* strictly adheres to presenting both 'the opinion and the other opinion," the network's policy is to balance any interview with individual speakers who represent each side of the story. Sadly, without a voice from the DoD, the network will find a voice from someone that may not always be the right voice for the DoD. At times, these political or military pundits may be seeking to further their own agenda vice the DoD's. Josh Rushing echoes this concern: "By refusing to submit to interviews or engage in debate on the network, the U.S. Government also deprives *Al Jazeera's* coverage and viewers of a balanced viewpoint, and instead allows the extreme positions of those on the left or the right to take over."[207] Further to that point, in a recent Twitter post, Rushing noted his frustration with the DoD's lack of responsiveness to his request for a spokesperson to appear on the program "The Stream" to address the issue of increasing incidents of sexual assault in the U.S. military. Rushing was aware the U.S. military had in fact adopted a zero tolerance policy and also implemented several positive measures to address this challenge. Therefore, in fairness to both the DoD and his viewers, he felt the program needed this information from a credible spokesperson from the DoD to truly represent the issue in its entirety. Unfortunately, the program aired on March 13, 2013 and noticeably absent was any voice or input from the DoD.[208] This example is only one of many examples in recent years that yet again, highlight the impact and consequences of our military's lack of responsiveness to requests for spokespersons for *Al Jazeera* programs.

Given the need to change this pattern, our senior leadership within the DoD and their PA teams, must be more proactive in responding to requests such as this and in scheduling other interviews as needed. If interviews are agreed upon, the interview(s) needs to be closely coordinated well in advance to ensure the focus and the boundaries are well-determined and defined. To be sure, the line of questioning on any *Al Jazeera* program will be difficult and could be wide-ranging including questions on broader U.S. Defense Strategy and U.S. Government policy. However, with adequate preparation and a firm understanding of what is expected from all parties, DoD's senior leaders and *Al Jazeera* can both achieve their desired goals from the interview. Key to this will be the willingness of *Al Jazeera* to work with the PA staff to ensure the expectations and guidelines for the interview are well understood in advance, especially for the initial interviews of the most senior DoD officials. Unfortunately, there have been times in the past when senior DoD leaders have been perceived to be "cut off" or "badgered" during interviews by *Al Jazeera* reporters, resulting in what appears to be very hostile interviews.[209] An interview that appears to be hostile could potentially set the relationship back and risk further support of interviews by the DoD and its senior leaders. Following the interview (s), senior leaders can determine the benefits of the engagement with their PA staff and provide feedback to the *Al Jazeera* senior leaders on their experience.

The positive example and proactive approach our senior leadership takes to improve the relationship with *Al Jazeera* can also serve as a broader engagement strategy for subordinate leaders across the military services. A good example is the U.S. Navy's willingness to support a request to interview the Chief of Naval Operations, Admiral Jonathan Greenert in March 2012 to discuss the U.S. Navy's capacity to secure the Strait of Hormuz if required. Greenert, who was attending the Middle East Naval Commander's Conference in Doha at that time, was clearly able to articulate the U.S. Navy's capacity to secure the Strait, and perhaps more importantly also reinforced the U.S. Government's commitment and resolve to do so.[210] To reinforce the message and commitment to security in the Persian Gulf and in the wake of Greenert's interview, the U.S. Navy and USCENTCOM decided to include *Al Jazeera-English* on a media embed with the U.S. Navy's Fifth Fleet on the USS Dwight D Eisenhower in September 2012.[211] Greenert's willingness to conduct the interview and the U.S. Navy's willingness to reach out to *Al Jazeera* for their participation onboard the carrier during the conduct of the massive training exercise, demonstrated the type of approach the rest of the services should take when afforded similar opportunities. This proactive approach sets the proper tone for service-wide engagement while also opening up other opportunities for other commands and leaders.

Additionally, the DoD and the respective services need to better empower subordinate leaders with the ability to conduct similar outreach and engagement with *Al Jazeera* and its various channels. Although the stories may not always be fully supportive of the DoD or the U.S. Government's policies, participating in the dialogue and discussion at least presents the key facts and data to support the respective DoD or U.S. Government position. Whether deployed or in garrison/port, there are countless stories of interest to the *Al Jazeera* networks, especially *Al Jazeera-America* and *Al Jazeera-English* as they seek to better interact with, appeal to and represent the American public. What better way to achieve this, than to highlight stories that deal with military or Veteran issues. As for operational and forward deployed leaders, the respective task force public affairs teams need to establish a routine engagement strategy with *Al Jazeera* in advance of the deployment, maintain routine contact during the deployment and look for follow up opportunities following the deployment.

Given the example presented earlier of a small team established within Dubai for maintaining engagement with the Arab networks, an equally effective method would be to build public affairs hubs that are interconnected with DoD that can provide both rapid response to unfolding news queries as well as the authorities to speak on the record if the story is based on the presentation of time sensitive information. Given the interconnectedness of the U.S. military and the technologies that are now available, it would be prudent to consider building a similar capacity as the 2006-2007 Dubai media team, within the growing number of regional media hubs currently being maintained by the U.S. State Department. If manning is an issue, then at a minimum providing one senior DoD public affairs professional at the media hubs, who is authorized to speak on behalf of the DoD would greatly assist in meeting the demands of global news networks like *Al Jazeera*, but would also assist the State Department in better understanding the situation and issues surrounding various U.S. military operations. Recognizing that this approach should not be exclusive to *Al Jazeera*, Professor Seib also suggests the U.S. DoD should "look at other growing trends in the Middle East namely engagement with *Al Arabiya*, the largest competitor to *Al Jazeera* in the Middle East. In addition to *Al Jazeera*, *Al Arabiya* offers a huge audience that includes many who consider *Al Jazeera* to be too radical in its political outlook. Beyond these two giants, among the byproducts of "the Arab Spring" has been substantial growth of local independent television channels. This development should be closely monitored by U.S. Government officials and use of these new channels should be incorporated in any U.S. Government media strategy."[212]

Finally, in Secretary of Defense Chuck Hagel's first remarks to the Pentagon, he highlighted the importance of international engagement by stating: "We can't dictate to the world, but we must engage with the world. That engagement in the world should be done wisely. And the resources that we employ on behalf of our country and our allies should always be applied wisely."[213] Given *Al Jazeera's* growing audience, global presence, and greater influence, the network provides a viable alternative to the other global networks operating in today's media landscape. Perhaps greater engagement with arguably the world's fastest growing and most strategically influential news network would meet the Secretary's intent of greater international engagement and meet his definition of a wise investment. To continue on the same path as the one our senior

DoD leaders have followed in recent years, meets neither his intent nor the definition of a wise investment.

Chapter V: Conclusion

As our military faces certain budget cuts and forces become more "globally responsive", it will be incumbent upon our leaders to ensure the world understands our efforts. As the face on the front lines of America's National Security Strategy, the U.S. military can be seen as an agent of occupation or an ambassador for good depending on what is communicated to the rest of the world. Whether in words or deeds, we must seek out opportunities to better educate and inform global audiences both in times of peace and in war. Embracing a culture of engagement with global news networks like *Al Jazeera*, symbolizes a willingness to listen and a willingness to learn; both of which are qualities America has often espoused, but in recent years has failed to follow. The findings of this research and recommendations contained herein are provided for consideration. Hopefully this research will serve as a catalyst for renewed engagement by the DoD with *Al Jazeera*; a result that would be mutually beneficial for both organizations.

Endnotes

[1] The author wishes to give credit to Dr. Jon Arquilla, Chair of the Department of Defense Analysis at the Naval Postgraduate School for his pioneering work and study of "swarm tactics" and its applications to modern and future warfare. For further readings on Professor Arquilla's concepts of "swarm tactics", see Swarming & The Future of Conflict. Santa Monica, CA: Rand, 2000. Additional readings include: Insurgents, Raiders, and Bandits: How Masters of Irregular Warfare Have Shaped Our World. (Lanham, MD: The Rowman &Littlefield Publishing Group, 2011), 55-67. and "Killer Swarms," Foreign Policy, November 26, 2012, http://www.foreignpolicy.com/articles/2012/11/26/killer_swarms.

[2] Brian Stelter, "Al Jazeera Seeks a U.S. Voice where Gore Failed," *The New York Times*, January 2, 2013.

[3] Press Release, "Al Jazeera to Start New US based Channel," *Al Jazeera*, January 2, 2013, http://www.aljazeerausannouncement.com/ (accessed January 23, 2013).

[4] Vivian Salama, "Al Jazeera in America; With its purchase of Current TV, the broadcaster has wide access to the American market for the first time. But will audiences come?," *Columbia Journalism Review*. January 9, 2013, http://www.cjr.org/behind_the_news/al_jazeera_in_america.php?page=all (accessed January 23, 2013).

[5] Danna Harman, "Backstory: The royal couple that put Qatar on the map," *Christian Science Monitor*, March 5, 2007, http://www.csmonitor.com/2007/0305/p20s01-wome.html/%28page%29/2 (accessed January 24, 2013)..

[6] Naomi Sakr , *Satellite Realms: Transnational Television, Globalization & the Middle East* (London, I.B. Tauris Pub, 2001), 57.

[7] Shawn Powers, "The Origins of Al Jazeera English" in Philip Seib, ed., *Al Jazeera English: Global News in a Changing World*. (New York, NY: Palgrave MacMillan, 2006), 8.

[8] Mohammed El Nawaway and Adel Iskandar. *Al Jazeera (Cambridge, MA:* Westview Press*, 2003),* 32.

[9] Ibid, 9.

[10] "How to watch *Al Jazeera* English on TV," *Al Jazeera*, January 20, 2013 http://www.aljazeera.com/watchaje/ (accessed on January 22, 2013).

[11] Press Release, "Public Liberties and Human Rights," *Al Jazeera*, November 2, 2008, http://www.aljazeera.com/aboutus/2008/11/2008112114536780324.html (accessed January 22, 2013).

[12] Seib, *Al Jazeera English: Global News in a Changing World*, 24.

[13] Philip M. Seib, e-mail message to author, February 27, 2013.

[14] "Al Jazeera Documentary Channel: List of Programs (Arabic)," *Al Jazeera*, tp://doc.aljazeera.net, (accessed January 25, 2013).

[15] Nick Vivarelli, "Deal brings toons, pix to Middle East and North Africa," *Variety*, March 11, 2013, http://variety.com/2013/tv/news/disney-content-to-air-on-al-jazeera-kids-channel-1200006822/ (accessed March 14, 2013).

[16] "Al Jazeera launches Balkans television channel," *BBC News*, January 11, 2011, http://www.bbc.co.uk/news/world-europe-15701549 (accessed January 25, 2013).

[17] Cengiz Semercio, "Diplomatic and Linguistic Roadblocks Keep Al Jazeera Turkish From Airing," *Al Hurriyet*. April 8, 2012, http://www.worldcrunch.com/source-partner/culture-society/diplomatic-and-linguistic-roadblocks-keep-al-jazeera-turkish-from-airing/c3s5043/#.ULEGg4fJQbR (accessed January 25, 2013)

[18] Danny Schecter, “Next steps for Al Jazeera America,” *Al Jazeera*, January 23, 2013, http://www.aljazeera.com/indepth/opinion/2013/01/2013120143533845915.html (accessed January 26, 2013).

[19] Press Release, “Al Jazeera to Start New US based Channel,” January 2, 2013.

[20] Phil Mushnick, “Gore’s Al Jazeera sale suspect,” *New York Post.* January 13, 2013.

[21] Jobs at Al Jazeera, “USA announcement,” *Al Jazeera*, http://www.aljazeerausannouncement.com/jobs.html (accessed January 26, 2013).

[22] "Check out Al Jazeera Media and Training Development Center’s 2011 courses," *Peace and Collaborative Development Network*, January 25, 2011, http://www.internationalpeaceandconflict.org/forum/topics/check-out-aljazeera-media (accessed January 24, 2013).

[23] “Current News and Reports,” *Al Jazeera Center for Studies*, http://studies.aljazeera.net/en/ (accessed January 26, 2013).

[24] Brian Stelter, “From Guantánamo to Desk at Al Jazeera,” *The New York Times,* December 22, 2009.

[25] Press Release, “Public Liberties and Human Rights,” *Al Jazeera*, November 2, 2008.

[26] Press Packet: “Purchase of Current TV,” *Al Jazeera*, January 3, 2013, 11, http://www.aljazeerausannouncement.com/Al-Jazeera-Purchase-of-Current-TV.pdf (accessed January 20, 2013)

[27] “Al Jazeera Facts and Figures,” *Al Jazeera*, February 23 2012, http://www.aljazeera.com/aboutus/2010/11/20101110131438787482.html (accessed January 12, 2013)

[28] Danny Schecter, “Next steps for Al Jazeera America,” *Al Jazeera*, January 23, 2013.

[29] “Al Jazeera 10 year anniversary key moments and data,” *Al Jazeera*, http://www.aljazeera.com/archive/2006/11/2008410115625813175.html (accessed January 17, 2013).

[30] “You Tube Top 100 Most Viewed News and Politics Video Producers,” *VidStatsX*, as of January 18, 2013, http://vidstatsx.com/youtube-top-100-most-viewed-news-politics (accessed January 18, 2013).

[31] Press Packet: “Purchase of Current TV”, January 3, 2013.

[32] Data taken from *Al Jazeera Network* hosted *Facebook* and *Twitter* sites on January 27, 2013. Al Jazeera programming was 8.7 million Facebook likes with additional likes on some of their other smaller network channels sites. Twitter followers for Al Jazeera and Al Jazeera English were 2.3 million and 1.5 million respectively. An additional .5 million Twitter followers could be found on the additional Al Jazeera channel Twitter sites.

[33] Comparison of *Al Jazeera-English* and *CNN International Twitter* accounts, https://twitter.com/AJEnglish (accessed March 6, 2013).

[34] James Wright and Patty Culhane of *Al Jazeera-English*, interview by author, September 19, 2013.

[35] El Nawaway and Iskandar, *Al Jazeera*, 33.

[36] Edmund Ghareeb, "New Media and the Information Revolution in the Arab World: An Assessment", Middle East Journal, Vol. 54, No. 3, The Information Revolution (Summer, 2000), 406.

[37] El Nawaway and Iskandar, *Al Jazeera, 23.*

[38] For background on the Muslim Brotherhood, see John L. Esposito, *The Islamic Threat: Myth or Reality?* (New York: Oxford University Press, 1992), 120-33.

[39] "Arab Satellite Television: The World through their eyes," *The Economist*, February 24, 2005, http://www.economist.com/node/3690442 (accessed 27 January, 2013).

[40] http://www.cbsnews.com/stories/2001/10/10/60minutes/main314278.shtml (Retrieved March 2, 2013)

[41] Marc Lynch, *Voices of the New Arab Public: Iraq, Al Jazeera, and Middle East Politics Today* (New York, NY: Columbia University Press, 2006), 2-3.

[42] Lawrence Pintak, "Arab Media and the Al Jazeera Effect," in *Global Communication: Theories, Stakeholders, and Trends,* ed. Thomas McPhail (Malden, MA: Wiley-Blackwell Publishing, 2010), 294.

[43] "Inside *Al Jazeera,*" *CBS News:60 Minutes*, February 11, 2009, http://www.cbsnews.com/stories/2001/10/10/60minutes/main314278.shtml (accessed January 23, 2013).

[44] El Nawaway and Iskandar, *Al Jazeera,* 23.

[45] Andrew Hammond, "Egypt seeks to block Al Jazeera's coverage," *Reuters*, January 30, 2011, http://www.torontosun.com/news/world/2011/01/30/17089226.html (accessed March 2, 2013).

[46] Regan Doherty, "Special Report: Al Jazeera's news revolution," *Reuters*, February 17, 2011, http://www.reuters.com/article/2011/02/17/us-aljazeera-idUSTRE71G0WC20110217 (accessed March 4, 2013).

[47] Ibid.

[48] Pintak, "Arab Media and the Al Jazeera Effect," in *Global Communication: Theories, Stakeholders, and Trends*, 296.

[49] Seib, e-mail, February 27, 2013.

[50] Doherty, "Special Report: Al Jazeera's news revolution, February 17, 2011.

[51] Robert Booth, "WikiLeaks cables claim al-Jazeera changed coverage to suit Qatari foreign policy," *The Guardian*, December 5, 2010, http://www.guardian.co.uk/world/2010/dec/05/wikileaks-cables-al-jazeera-qatari-foreign-policy (accessed March 4, 2013).

[52] Doherty, "Special Report: Al Jazeera's news revolution, February 17, 2011. (According to Doherty: 'Initially, the channel's coverage of Saudi Arabia -- the Arab world's leading political and economic power -- was extensive, but in 2002 the kingdom withdrew its ambassador to Doha partly in protest over Al Jazeera shows on Saudi politics. Relations between the two states were restored six years later, and observers say Al Jazeera toned down its Saudi coverage."

[53] Booth, " WikiLeaks cables claim al-Jazeera changed coverage to suit Qatari foreign policy," December 5, 2010.

[54] Wissam Kanaan, *"Al Jazeera reporter resigns over "biased" Syria coverage,"* Alakhbar English, March 8, 2012, http://english.al-akhbar.com/print/4941 (accessed March 5, 2013).

[55] Ibid.

[56] Dan Sabbagh, "Al Jazeera's political independence questioned amid Qatar intervention," The Guardian, September 30, 2012, http://www.guardian.co.uk/media/2012/sep/30/al-jazeera-independence-questioned-qatar (accessed March 4, 2013).

[57] Doherty, "Special Report: Al Jazeera's news revolution, February 17, 2011.

[58] Ibid.

[59] Mohammad Mohammad, "*Al-Jazeera: Voice of the Voiceless*," University of Texas, course description, http://www.utexas.edu/ugs/sig/courses/descriptions?semester=77&format=5 (accessed February 24, 2013).

[60] "Al Jazeera English is Independent," *Parker-Spitzer*, CNN, Special Report, February 23, 2011.

[61] Hugh Miles, "Think Again: Al Jazeera," *Foreign Policy,* June 12, 2006.

[62] Ibid.

[63] El Nawaway and Iskandar, *Al Jazeera,* 52.

[64] Ibid, 53.

[65] Ibid, 53-54.

[66] Tony Rogers, "Is al Jazeera anti-Semitic and anti-American?," *About.com Journalism Guide*, http://journalism.about.com/od/trends/a/Is-Al-Jazeera-Anti-Semitic-And-Anti-American.htm (accessed November 6, 2012).

[67] Sharon Waxman, "Arab TV's Strong Signal: The al-Jazeera Network Offers News the Mideast Never Had Before, and Views That Are All Too Common," *Washington Post*, 4 December 2001.

[68] Timothy Groseclose, *Left Turn: How liberal media bias distorts the American mind* (New York, NY: St. Martin's Press, 2011), 155.

[69] William Youmans and Katie Brown, "Can Al Jazeera English leverage its 'Egypt Moment' into an American audience?" *Arab Media & Society* 13 (Spring): 2.

[70] Ibid.

[71] Doherty, "Special Report: Al Jazeera's news revolution, February 17, 2011.

[72] El Nawaway and Iskandar, *Al Jazeera,* 22.

[73] Hatem EL Zein, "The intersection of interests between Al Jazeera and Al Qaida in the era of "War on Terror," *Online Journal of Communication and Media Technologies,* October 2012, 177, http://www.ojcmt.net/articles/24/2410.pdf (accessed 13 January 2013).

[74] Marc Lynch, "Al Qaeda's Media Strategies," *The National Interest, (*Spring 2006):50, in ProQuest (accessed October 15, 2012).

[75] Alice Fordham, "Up next on Al Jazeera: Donald Rumsfeld," *Washington Post*, September 30, 2011.

[76] Cliff Kincaid, "Al Jazeera's Anti-American Bias," *Accuracy in Media*, June 23, 2004, http://www.aim.org/media-monitor/al-jazeeras-anti-american-bias (accessed October 26, 2012).

[77] Pintak, "Arab Media and the Al Jazeera Effect," in *Global Communication: Theories, Stakeholders, and Trends*, 293.

[78] El Nawaway and Iskandar, *Al Jazeera,*47.

[79] "Public Diplomacy and U.S. Foreign Policy: The 1997-1998 Iraq Crisis," *United States Information Agency's Public Diplomacy Forum*, April 8, 1998, http://dosfan.lib.uic.edu/usia/usiahome/pdforum/iraq.htm (accessed January 14, 2013).

[80] Will Youmans, "AJE after the Arab Spring: The Politics of Distribution in the United States" in Philip Seib, ed., *Al Jazeera English: Global News in a Changing World.* (New York, NY: Palgrave MacMillan, 2006), 61.

[81] El Nawaway and Iskandar, *Al Jazeera,*175.

[82] "Pakistan to Demand Taliban Give Up bin Laden as Iran Seals Afghan Border," *Fox News,* September 16, 2001, http://www.foxnews.com/story/0,2933,34440,00.html (accessed January 26, 2013).

[83] Pintak, "Arab Media and the Al Jazeera Effect," in *Global Communication: Theories, Stakeholders, and Trends*, 293.

[84] "Al-Jazeera Kabul offices hit in US raid," *BBC News,* November 13, 2001, http://news.bbc.co.uk/2/hi/south_asia/1653887.stm (accessed January 26, 2013)

[85] Jessica Goldings, "Al Jazeera Timeline," Pew Research Center's Project for Excellence in Journalism, August 22, 2006, http://www.journalism.org/node/1529 (accessed January 27 2013).

[86] "American Wrath Unleashed on Afghanistan," *Agence France Presse,* October 7, 2001, http://www.commondreams.org/headlines01/1007-03.htm (accessed January 25, 2013).

[87] El Nawaway and Iskandar, *Al Jazeera,*176.

[88] "TV station defends bin Laden coverage," *BBC News,* October 10, 2001, http://news.bbc.co.uk/2/hi/middle_east/1591361.stm (accessed January 26, 2013).

[89] "Al-Jazeera Kabul offices hit in US raid," *BBC News,* November 13, 2001.

[90] Brian Stelter, "From Guantánamo to Desk at Al Jazeera," *The New York Times,* December 22, 2009, A13.

[91] "Iraq Broadcasts Images of Five U.S. Prisoners of War," *PBS News Hour,* March 23, 2003, http://www.pbs.org/newshour/updates/prisoners_03-23-03.html (accessed January 26, 2013).

[92] Ibid.

[93] Jeremy M. Sharp, The Al-Jazeera News Network: Opportunity or Challenge for U.S. Foreign Policy in the Middle East? (Washington, DC: U.S. Library of Congress, Congressional Research Service, July 23, 2003), 7.

[94] Ibid.

[95] Joyce Purnic, "Metro Matters; Censorship Is Patriotism To Big Board," *The New York Times,* March 27, 2003, http://www.nytimes.com/2003/03/27/nyregion/metro-matters-censorship-is-patriotism-to-big-board.html?pagewanted=1 (accessed January 27, 2013).

[96] Ibid.

[97] Ibid.

[98] Thomas S. Mulligan, "Nasdaq Joins in Ban of Al Jazeera," *Los Angeles Times,* March 26, 2003, http://articles.latimes.com/2003/mar/26/news/war-banned26 (accessed January 26, 2013).

[99] Sharp, The Al-Jazeera News Network: Opportunity or Challenge for U.S. Foreign Policy in the Middle East?, 7.

[100] Jason Deans, "Al Jazeera's Basra hotel bombed," *The Guardian*, April 2, 2003, http://www.guardian.co.uk/media/2003/apr/02/broadcasting.iraq1 (accessed January 23, 2013).

[101] "Al Jazeera hit by missile," BBC News, April 8, 2003, http://news.bbc.co.uk/2/hi/middle_east/2927527.stm (accessed January 23, 2013).

[102] Deans, "Al Jazeera's Basra hotel bombed," *The Guardian*, April 2, 2003.

[103] "U.S. Bombing Raid Kills Three Journalists in Baghdad," *Fox News,* April 8, 2003, http://www.foxnews.com/story/0,2933,83503,00.html#ixzz2OPKOjHdg (accessed January 26, 2013).

[104] Dima Tareq Tahboub, "The war on Al Jazeera: The US is determined to suppress the independent Arab media," *The Guardian*, October 3, 2003, http://www.guardian.co.uk/world/2003/oct/04/iraq.iraqandthemedia (accessed January 24, 2013).

[105] "Al Jazeera in the Crosshairs: Did Bush Really Want to Bomb the Arabic TV Network's Headquarters in 2004?," *Democracy Now*, November 29, 2005, http://www.democracynow.org/2005/11/29/al_jazeera_in_the_crosshairs_did (accessed January 26, 2013).

[106] Nora Boustany, "For Al Jazeera, Loss of Convention Sign Brings Banner Publicity," *Washington Post*, July 28, 2004, http://www.washingtonpost.com/wp-dyn/articles/A19359-2004Jul27.html (accessed January 13, 2013).

[107] "American fakes own decapitation in tape," *Associated Press,* August 7, 2004, http://www.nbcnews.com/id/5629119/ (accessed January 14, 2013).

[108] Judea Pearl, "Another Perspective, or Jihad TV?," *The New York Times,* January 17, 2007, http://www.nytimes.com/2007/01/17/opinion/17pearl.html?pagewanted=all (accessed January 14, 2013).

[109] Wolf Blitzer Reports Staff, "Al Jazeera's Baghdad office closed for 30 days," August 9, 2004, http://articles.cnn.com/2004-08-09/us/aljazeera.baghdad_1_al-jazeera-s-baghdad-al-jazeera-s-washington-hafez-al-mirazi?_s=PM:US (accessed January 21, 2013).

[110] Ibid.

[111] Ibid.

[112] Luke Harding, "Iraq extends Al Jazeera ban and raids offices," The Guardian, September 6, 2004, http://www.guardian.co.uk/media/2004/sep/06/iraq.broadcasting (accessed January 25, 2013).

[113] Mark Finkelstein, "Even Al Jazeera Sees Improvement in Baghdad Situation," *CNS News,* March 8, 2007, http://bsimmons.wordpress.com/2007/03/08/even-al-jazeera-sees-improvement-in-baghdad-situation/ (accessed January 24, 2013).

[114] "Al-Jazeera allowed back in Baghdad," *Agence France Presse*, March 4, 2011, http://www.news.com.au/breaking-news/al-jazeera-allowed-back-in-baghdad/story-e6frfku0-1226015684471#ixzz1GAwAbqii (accessed January 24, 2013).

[115] "Bomb Jazeera memo: Media warned," *CNN International,* November 24, 2005, http://edition.cnn.com/2005/WORLD/europe/11/23/britain.jazeera/ (accessed January 24, 2013).

[116] Ibid.

[117] "Secrets-leaker handed prison term," Reuters, May 10, 2007, http://uk.reuters.com/article/2007/05/10/uk-britain-trial-secrets-idUKL1060345320070510 (accessed January 24, 2013).

[118] Youmans, *Al Jazeera English: Global News in a Changing World,* 61.

[119] "Al Jazeera's Global Gamble: A PEJ Interview, Al Jazeera Timeline" *Pew Research Center's Project for Excellence in Journalism*, August 22, 2006, http://www.journalism.org/node/1530 (accessed January 26, 2013).

[120] "Interview with Wadah Khanfar, Director General, Al Jazeera," *PBS Frontline World News*, March 27, 2007, http://www.pbs.org/frontlineworld/stories/newswar/war_interviews.html (accessed January 23, 2013).

[121] "Frost over the World," *YouTube,* November 2, 2007, http://www.youtube.com/watch?v=oIO8B6fpFSQ (accessed January 26, 2013).

[122] Josh Rushing, *Mission Al Jazeera: Build a Bridge, Seek the Truth, Change the World* (New York: Palgrave MacMillan, 2007), 98-99.

[123] Ibid., 153.

[124] "Obama tells Al Arabiya peace talks should resume," *Al Arabiya News,* January 27, 2009, http://www.alarabiya.net/articles/2009/01/27/65087.html (accessed January 23, 2013).

[125] Kincaid, "Al Jazeera's Anti-American Bias," *Accuracy in Media*, June 23, 2004.

[126] Pamela Geller, "Al Jazeera tries to whitewash bloody record," *Atlas Shrugs,* entry posted March 3, 2013, http://atlasshrugs2000.typepad.com/atlas_shrugs/al-jazeera-jihad-tv-in-america/ (accessed march 21, 2013).

[127] "Hillary Clinton Calls Al Jazeera 'Real News,' Criticizes U.S. Media," Huffington Post, March 3, 2011, http://www.huffingtonpost.com/2011/03/03/hillary-clinton-calls-al-_n_830890.html (accessed January 23, 2013).

[128] "Clinton Meets With Al Jazeera Brass In Qatar," *The Huffington Post,* April 17, 2010, http://www.huffingtonpost.com/2010/02/15/clintonmeets-with-al-jaz_n_463050.html (accessed January 13, 2013).

[129] Keach Hagey and Byron Tau, "Al Jazeera has fans in Obama W.H.," *Politico,* April 17, 2011, http://www.politico.com/news/stories/0411/53339.html#ixzz2OlyIpvwi (accessed January 25, 2013).

[130] Ibid.

[131] "John McCain speaks at the Al Jazeera US Forum," *You Tube,* May 24, 2011, http://www.youtube.com/watch?v=GMq5P7j13ZY (accessed January 24, 2013).

[132] "Pelosi, McCain salute Al Jazeera," *Politico,* May 17, 2011, http://www.politico.com/blogs/onmedia/0511/Pelosi_McCain_salute_Al_Jazeera.html (accessed January 24, 2013).

[133] Laura Collins-Hughes, "An Al Jazeera fan, sent by Colin Powell," *Boston Globe*, February 15, 2011, http://www.boston.com/ae/specials/culturedesk/2011/02/an_al_jazeera_fan_sent_by_coli.html (accessed on January 23, 2013).

[134] "Colin Powell: Talk to Al Jazeera", *Al Jazeera*, September 19, 2001, http://www.aljazeera.com/programmes/talktojazeera/2011/09/201191993444637938.html (accessed January 23, 2013).

[135] Alice Fordham, "Up next on al-Jazeera: Donald Rumsfeld," *Washington Post*, September 30, 2011, http://www.washingtonpost.com/blogs/checkpoint-washington/post/up-next-on-al-jazeera-donald-rumsfeld/2011/09/29/gIQA1d0O8K_blog.html (accessed January 21, 2013).

[136] "Public Diplomacy and U.S. Foreign Policy: The 1997-1998 Iraq Crisis," http://dosfan.lib.uic.edu/usia/usiahome/pdforum/iraq.htm (accessed January 14, 2013).

[137] Riz Khan, "Love in Black and White," *Al Jazeera-English*, December 18, 2007, http://www.aljazeera.com/programmes/rizkhan/2007/12/2008525185959646819.html

[138] Brian Bennett, "U.S. Mends Frosty Relations with Al Jazeera," *Los Angeles Times*, February 7, 2011, http://articles.latimes.com/2011/feb/07/world/la-fg-al-jazeera-20110207 (accessed January 23, 2013).

[139] "Secretary Rumsfeld Interview With Al Jazeera TV," *U.S. Department of Defense*, Office of the Assistant Secretary of Defense (Public Affairs) News Transcript, February 25, 2003, http://www.defense.gov/transcripts/transcript.aspx?transcriptid=1946 (accessed January 23, 2013).

[140] Bootie Cosgrove-Mather, "FTN – 3/23/03- Part 1," *CBS News,* Transcript of interview with Donald Rumsfeld, posted February 11, 2009, http://www.cbsnews.com/8301-3460_162-545616.html (accessed January 24, 2013).

[141] "Aljazeera slams Rumsfeld 'terror' slur," *Al Jazeera,* September 15, 2004, http://www.aljazeera.com/archive/2004/09/200849135117322239.html (accessed January 24, 2013).

[142] "Al Jazeera Banned From Iraq," *TVNZ,* September 5, 2004, http://tvnz.co.nz/content/445873/425822/article.html (accessed January 28, 2013).

[143] Rushing, *Mission Al Jazeera: Build a Bridge, Seek the Truth, Change the World*, 174.

[144] Ibid, 176.

[145] "British journalist freed in Iraq," *Agence France Presse,* January 15, 2006, http://www.theage.com.au/news/world/british-journalist-freed-in-iraq/2006/01/15/1137119014679.html (accessed January 23, 2013).

[146] Brian Witte, "Gates: Congress, Press Not the Enemy," *The Associated Press,* May 25, 2007, http://www.washingtonpost.com/wp-dyn/content/article/2007/05/25/AR2007052501128.html (accessed January 21, 2013).

[147] "Interview: Robert Gates," *Al Jazeera,* September 7, 2009, http://www.aljazeera.com/news/americas/2009/09/200995202939732522.html (accessed January 27, 2013).

[148] "Robert Gates interview," *Al Jazeera,* June 10, 2010, http://www.aljazeera.com/programmes/frostovertheworld/2010/06/201061091243602584.html (accessed January 27, 2013).

[149] Author's personal memoirs and experiences while assigned to Multi-National Force-Iraq as a communication specialist and advisor to the Chief Spokesman, Maj Gen. William B. Caldwell, IV. September 2006-May 2007.

[150] Caitlin Huey-Burns, "10 Things You Didn't Know About Mike Mullen," *US News and World Report,* March 28, 2011, http://www.usnews.com/news/articles/2011/03/28/10-things-you-didnt-know-about-mike-mullen (accessed January 26, 2013).

[151] James Dao, "Pentagon Keeps Wary Watch as Troops Blog," *The New York Times,* September 8, 2009, http://www.nytimes.com/2009/09/09/us/09milblogs.html?_r=1&adxnnlx=1252584080-vptPSyOQ4tllOV5Lhq5UbQ&pagewanted=all (accessed January 23, 2013).

[152] "Q&A: US Admiral Michael Mullen," *Al Jazeera,* July 23, 2009, http://www.aljazeera.com/focus/2009/07/200972253325298956.html (accessed January 24, 2013).

[153] "Afghan War: The Exit Strategy," *Al Jazeera-You Tube Channel,* December 3, 2009, https://www.youtube.com/watch?v=AcyYtZXQpGQ (accessed January 24, 2013).

[154] James Wright and Patty Culhane of Al Jazeera English, interview by author, Washington, DC, September 19, 2012.

[155] Ben Fox and Alfred de Montesquiou, "Al-Jazeera Cameraman Still at Guantanamo," The Associated Press, February 23, 2007, http://web.archive.org/web/20070228100307/http://www.guardian.co.uk/worldlatest/story/0,,-6435812,00.html (accessed January 21, 2013).

[156] Rushing, *Mission Al Jazeera: Build a Bridge, Seek the Truth, Change the World*, 173.

[157] William B. Caldwell, IV, "Remarks to the National Editorial Writer's Convention," question and answer commentary, Kansas City, MO, Westin Crown Center, September 27, 2007,

http://usacac.army.mil/cac2/repository/SelectedSpeeches/NEWC.pdf (accessed January 25, 2013).

[158] "Talk to Al Jazeera : William Caldwell: Leaving Afghanistan," *Al Jazeera,* December 3, 2011, http://www.youtube.com/watch?v=wT_hWIPqeQ0 (accessed January 23, 2013).

[159] Marc Ambinder, "How Al Jazeera Outlasted Donald Rumsfeld," *The Atlantic,* December 10, 2009, http://www.theatlantic.com/politics/archive/2009/12/how-al-jazeera-outlasted-donald-rumsfeld/31587/ (accessed January 23, 2013).

[160] Ibid.

[161] Peter Johnson, "U.S. says Al-Jazeera putting troops at risk," *USA Today*, April 18, 2004, http://usatoday30.usatoday.com/life/columnist/mediamix/2004-04-18-media-mix_x.htm (accessed January 26, 2013).

[162] Marc Lynch, "Mark Kimmitt on al-Jazeera," *Abu Aardvark,* April 13, 2006, http://abuaardvark.typepad.com/abuaardvark/2006/04/kimmett_on_alja.html (accessed January 25, 2013).

[163] While assigned to NATO Training Mission-Afghanistan from August 2010 until November 2011, the author noted countless examples of senior leaders choosing to watch AJ-English (AJE) as opposed to CNN or BBC as had been the dominant cable television choices during previous deployment to Iraq in 2006 and 2007.

[164] Personal meeting with Commanding General and Deputies, NATO Training Mission Afghanistan. February 12, 2011.

[165] A comprehensive review of each of the senior leader's Wikipedia and personal social media pages on January 24, 2013 highlighted the disparity in the number of television appearances on U.S. domestic-based networks, namely CNN as well as BBC. Notably absent was any appearance on any of the *Al Jazeera* channels other than Admiral Greenert, CNO.

[166] Wright and Culhane, interview by author, September 19, 2012.

[167] Camille El Hassani, e-mail message to author, December 7, 2012.

[168] Wright and Culhane, interview, September 19, 2012.

[169] Confidential interviews of senior public affairs officials within DoD and senior officers, who asked not to be quoted directly. Interviews conducted in Washington, DC, September 13-15, 2012.

[170] U.S. Joint Chiefs of Staff, *Public Affairs*, Joint Publication 3-61 (Washington, DC: U.S. Joint Chiefs of Staff, August 25, 2010), I-1.

[171] Ibid, I-8.

[172] Dr. Hy Rothstein, Department of Defense Analysis, U.S Naval Postgraduate School, interview by author, Monterey, CA, November 20, 2012.

[173] Interviews. September 13-15, 2012.

[174] Meeting notes, NATO Training Mission Afghanistan. February 2011.

[175] "Chuck Hagel on US foreign policy," Al Jazeera, April 1, 2009, http://www.aljazeera.com/programmes/rizkhan/2009/03/200933174623720671.html (accessed March 28, 2013).

[176] General Martin E. Dempsey, U.S. Chairman of the Joint Chiefs of Staff, *Capstone Concept for Joint Operations: Joint Force 2020* (Washington, DC: U.S. Department of Defense, September 2012), 3.

[177] U.S. Office of Management and Budget, *Budget of the United States Government, Fiscal Year 2013* (Washington, DC: U.S. Government Printing Office, 2012), 3.

[178] CNN Worldwide Fact Sheet, http://cnnpressroom.blogs.cnn.com/cnn-fact-sheet/ (accessed January 30 2013)

[179] Al Jazeera Press Packet: Purchase of Current TV. Dated January 3, 2013. P. 11.

[180] Neal Ungerleider (9 February 2011). "Al Jazeera, Stymied in U.S., Launching Turkish-Only Channel". Fast Company. http://www.fastcompany.com/1725643/al-jazeera-stymied-us-launching-turkish-only-channel. Retrieved 18 January 2013.

[181] Philip Seib, *The Al Jazeera Effect: How the New Global Media Are Reshaping World Politics* (Washington, DC: Potomac Books, 2008), 15.

[182] Jesse Holcomb, Amy Mitchell and Tom Rosentiel, The State of the News Media 2012, "*Cable: CNN Ends Its Ratings Slide, Fox Falls Again*", March 19, 2012, http://stateofthemedia.org/2012/cable-cnn-ends-its-ratings-slide-fox-falls-again/#cnn-refining-its-identity (accessed January 14, 2013).

[183] Tine Ustad Figenschou, "A Voice for the Voiceless? A Quantitative Content Analysis of Al Jazeera English's Flagship News," *Global Media Communication* 6 (2010): 91-98.

[184] Barack H. Obama, President of the United States, *Sustaining U.S. Global Leadership: Priorities for 21st Century Defense.* (Washington, DC: The White House, January 3,2012), cover letter, 1.

[185] James Wright, e-mail message to author, February 27, 2013.

[186] Anthony A. Maalouf, "The Influence of Al Jazeera in the Arab World and the Response of Arab Governments", Thesis, Villanova University, May 2008, 7, in ProQuest (accessed January 27, 2013).

[187] El Nawaway, *Al Jazeera, 23.*

[188] Pew Research Center, Global Attitudes Project, June 13, 2012, page 1.

[189] Philip Auter, Mohamed M. Arafa, and Khaled Al-Jaber, "Who Is Al Jazeera's Audience? Deconstructing the Demographics and Psychographics of an Arab Satellite News Network," *Journal of Transnational Broadcasting Studies* 12, (Spring-Summer 2004): http://www.tbsjournal.com/auter.htm (accessed 28 January 2013).

[190] Lydia Saad, 2002 Gallup Poll of the Islamic World, "Al Jazeera Viewers Perceive West Differently", April 23, 2002, http://www.gallup.com/poll/5860/AlJazeera-Viewers-Perceive-West-Differently.aspx, (accessed December 22, 2012).

[191] Dr. Glenn Robinson of the Department of Defense Analysis, U.S Naval Postgraduate School, interview by author, Monterey, CA, January 30, 2013.

[192] El Nawaway, *Al Jazeera,*44.

[193] Rushing, *Mission Al Jazeera: Build a Bridge, Seek the Truth, Change the World*, 135.

[194] "Corporate profile," Al Jazeera-English, April 16, 2012, http://m.aljazeera.com/home/about (accessed January 21, 2013).

[195] Youmans, *Al Jazeera English: Global News in a Changing World,* 63.

[196] Seib, *The Al Jazeera Effect: How the New Global Media Are Reshaping World Politics*, 175.

[197] Youmans, *Al Jazeera English: Global News in a Changing World,* 63.

[198] "Awards won by Al Jazeera English," *Al Jazeera*, March 28, 2013, http://www.aljazeera.com/pressoffice/2012/04/2012416161854868952.html (accessed March 31, 2013).

[199] "Columbia University Awards Top Journalism Prize to Al Jazeera English," Fox News, May 5, 2011, http://www.foxnews.com/us/2011/05/05/al-jazeera-english-wins-columbia-universitys-journalism-prize/ (accessed march 31, 2013).

[200] Ibid.

[201] Rushing, *Mission Al Jazeera: Build a Bridge, Seek the Truth, Change the World*, 161.

[202] Alfred Fletcher Conard, *Costs of Administering Reparation for Work Injuries in Illinois* (Champaign, IL, 1952), 28.

[203] "Clinton Meets With Al Jazeera Brass In Qatar," *The Huffington Post*, April 17, 2010.

[204] Interviews. September 13-15, 2012.

[205] Author's personal accounts and comments reflected in "Executive Trip Summary: Commanding General, NATO Training Mission-Afghanistan," Doha, Qatar. October 19, 2011.

[206] Ibid.

[207] Rushing, *Mission Al Jazeera: Build a Bridge, Seek the Truth, Change the World*, 157.

[208] "Confronting military rape culture," *Al Jazeera's "The Stream",* March 13, 2013, http://stream.aljazeera.com/story/201303130043-0022608 (accessed March 15, 2013).

[209] "Rumsfeld in heated conversation with Al Jazeera," *You Tube-Al Jazeera English,* October 4, 2011, http://www.youtube.com/watch?v=tiTaAh0W5Is (accessed March 21, 2013).

[210] "US Navy capable of securing Strait of Hormuz," *You Tube-Al Jazeera English,* March 26, 2012, http://www.youtube.com/watch?v=U27vk0AyHNY (accessed March 13, 2013).

[211] Cal Perry, "On board the USS Eisenhower, September 23, 2012, http://www.aljazeera.com/indepth/inpictures/2012/09/2012923152342729444.html, (accessed January 28, 2013).

[212] Seib, e-mail, February 27, 2013.

[213] Craig Whitlock, "Hagel Vows Straight Talk, Loyalty to Troops," *Washington Post,* February 28, 2013.

www.ingramcontent.com/pod-product-compliance
Lightning Source LLC
Chambersburg PA
CBHW080311290526
45790CB00005B/1999

9781511465823